Patina

How to Create & Preserve

Kevin Tetz

CarTech®

CarTech®

CarTech®, Inc.
838 Lake Street South
Forest Lake, MN 55025
Phone: 651-277-1200 or 800-551-4754
Fax: 651-277-1203
www.cartechbooks.com

Edit by Wes Eisenschenk
Layout by Monica Seiberlich

ISBN 978-1-61325-467-7
Item No. SA447

Library of Congress Cataloging-in-Publication Data
Names: Tetz, Kevin, 1963- author.
Title: Patina : how to create & preserve / Kevin Tetz.
Description: Forest Lake, MN : CarTech, [2019]
Identifiers: LCCN 2018043915 | ISBN 9781613254677
Subjects: LCSH: Automobiles–Painting. | Automobiles–Bodies–Maintenance and repair.
Classification: LCC TL255.2 .T425 2019 | DDC 629.2/60288–dc23
LC record available at https://lccn.loc.gov/2018043915

Images used under license from shutterstock.com on pages 8, 9, 10, 45, 51, and 52.
Written, edited, and designed in the U.S.A.
Printed in China
10 9 8 7 6 5 4 3 2 1

CarTech books may be purchased at a discounted rate in bulk for resale, events, corporate gifts, or educational purposes. Special editions may also be created to specification.
For details, contact Special Sales at 838 Lake Street S., Forest Lake MN 55025 or by email at sales@cartechbooks.com.

DISTRIBUTION BY:

Europe
PGUK
63 Hatton Garden
London EC1N 8LE, England
Phone: 020 7061 1980 • Fax: 020 7242 3725
www.pguk.co.uk

Australia
Renniks Publications Ltd.
3/37-39 Green Street
Banksmeadow, NSW 2109, Australia
Phone: 2 9695 7055 • Fax: 2 9695 7355
www.renniks.com

Canada
Login Canada
300 Saulteaux Crescent
Winnipeg, MB, R3J 3T2 Canada
Phone: 800 665 1148 • Fax: 800 665 0103
www.lb.ca

CONTENTS

ACKNOWLEDGMENTS

This work is dedicated to my wife and partner, Judy. Everything is possible with you by my side.

Special thanks to:

Ron Covell, for your unwavering support and friendship.

Uncle Herb Pinske, for opening my ears to the story that old cars tell.

My mom, Lynn Herrington, who is my precious inspiration.

My big brother, Blaine Tetz, who taught me to "never give up, never give in."

My father, Wes Tetz, for showing me that I'll never be unemployed if I know how to work.

Kevin Reynolds, for teaching me how to be a team player.

Howard and Sally Copeland, for their boundless love and support.

My industry friends and family . . . I'm so blessed and fortunate to have you on my side!

Another wonderful adventure is just around the corner!

1949 CHEVY 3100 HIGHLIGHT PROJECT

This 49 Chevrolet 3100 saw quite a transformation from the worn out original farm truck during the 7 episodes of TRUCKS! where we customized and restyled it. The suspension was lowered, engine and transmission rebuild and updated, headlights and taillights Frenched, the cab converted to a 5-window version, and a one-piece windshield installed. Missing now from my original version are the raw-copper grill, bumpers, and trim pieces, but the current owner has personalized it to his style and loves his version of this very cool truck. It's nice to see that several years later, and having changed hands several times the patina-paint is still serving the purpose of adding character to a classic truck.

WHAT IS PATINA?

The word *patina* means many things to many people. In the classic car world, patina is the new buzzword used to describe original wear and unmolested aging on factory parts. During the past several years, an entire category of classic car, called the "Survivor," has arisen as part of a preservation movement that carries the goal of saving the original and unrestored status of vehicles. The Survivor is now the high-water mark of automotive collectors, and finding and showcasing the original condition of a vehicle is much mo[re] important than restoring one to pri[s]tine condition.

I've spoken with several exper[ts] in the collector car world, and man[y] of them mentioned that not ver[y] long ago there were many veh[icles]

This early 1950s truck is all but reclaimed by nature, but it is a beautiful example of how nature will eventually take bac[k] its resources. Our job as artists and technicians is to slow the process of time as we restore cars and give tribute to mother nature by recreating the original appearance of patina.

es that underwent a complete res-ration when they were in good ough condition to be preserved survivor vehicles. Because of the storations, much of the history, eritage, and provenance of these hicles has been lost when it wasn't ally necessary. After all, patina is uch more than the faded and dull onze look of a Tiffany lamp sit-ng in a museum. Patina, as it relates the automotive hobby, is another ord for realism, and it brings with it thenticity.

ntage instruments have long been llected and revered for their patina d condition. It's a recent trend in struments, as well as classic cars, to yle the finish on insignificant guitars d other instruments to appear as eathered and worn finishes. Inter-stingly, the Fender guitar company as a special division of guitars lled their "relicked" line. Fender licked guitars bring many thou-nds of dollars more in sales price an a top-of-the-line instrument with premium finish, simply due to the erception that it is a vintage guitar. his is partially brought on by the sky-cketing prices of 1950s' and 1960s' ntage instruments in original condi-on. This guitar was relicked by a DIY ser, and it serves his purposes nicely a well-worn guitar that seems to ll a story.

Forms of Patina

Patina in the automotive context can refer to any fading, darkening, or other signs of age that are felt to be natural or unavoidable. Natural oxidation where patina forms or is deliberately induced is called patina-tion, and the definition can apply to naturally occurring or artist-rendered aging.

There are other forms of artist-rendered aging, or fauxtina. Distressed furniture is a form of faux patina, and relicked guitars and instruments are pre-aged. Faux-tina paint jobs create the illusion of weathered finish but bypass 40 to 60 years of naturally occurring oxidation in the elements. The patina on musi-cal instruments tell a particular story; the wear marks on fretboards, bodies,

Even something as utilitarian as a galvanized piece of sheet metal can show beautiful patina. The oxidation tells a story and gives us a color palate of muted but sophisticated tones and hues.

American guitar icon Stevie Ray Vaughan used to set a cigarette between the E-string and the headstock of his Fender Strat. He would get so caught up in playing that it would burn down and eventually burn out, staining the wood with heat and tobacco.

or tuning keys whisper of countless hours of play as well as provide clues to the history of the instrument and to the character of the owner. Stevie Ray Vaughan famously placed a cigarette under the strings of the tuning keys on his guitars, and you can see burn marks from the cigarette on many of the headstocks, making them authentic collector's items.

A well-preserved but slightly worn instrument can be worth far more than a refinished instrument of the same vintage. Fender guitars have a line of Stratocaster instruments that are individually customized to look like they were worn down by time. These guitars bring a much higher price than the new counterparts similarly equipped, which nods to the popularity of fauxtina as an art form.

There are wonderful television programs where people show off their family heirlooms and get a valuation from an expert who analyzes the condition and learns the history of these treasures. Qualified experts analyze the condition of these heirlooms based on the heritage, age, condition, and documentation, and they arrive at a fair market value that sometimes surprises the owner. Often there is a lamp, a statue, or even a painting that has been "repaired" or reconditioned, and the process of removing or repairing the original finish significantly devalued the object. Patina is king! Leave your Tiffany lamp alone and don't even polish it. It is much better to have patina with antiques than to have a fixed-up version of the same thing.

One of Merriam-Webster's definitions of patina is: a surface appearance of something grown beautiful especially with age or use. The other definition refers to aging on bronze metals, which we'll discuss briefly, but the real subject of this book is to show you how to create authentic-looking patina and the look of natural aging on many different surfaces. Ultimately, you have to decide whether to preserve valuable original patina, add to some naturally occurring age, or start with a totally clean palate and create your own version of Fauxtina.

History of Fauxtina

Manipulating naturally occurring oxidation and aging to gain a desired effect is nothing new. In fact, styled patina has been used for centuries to accentuate statues and sculptures including adding color to lips, eyes and armor. The bronze statues of the 19th century had alloy blends that dictated the color and brightness of the bronze itself. However, different chemicals have been applied over the ages to tint and accent these works of art.

The traditional green accent in many bronze works has been accepted as "natural" patina for many years, but recent studies show that large quantities of sulfur introduced into the atmosphere during the Industrial Revolution of the late 1700s gave a distinctly greenish appearance to outdoor bronze statues. This is a byproduct of industrial fallout and pollution much more than it is a natural reaction between metal and atmosphere, so even in the traditional sense "patina" is arguably

This bronze statue of Leonidas has a uniform patina overall, but it's now believed that in Roman times these statues were decorated with lifelike colors on the clothing, facial features, and weapons. The colors were a product of chemistry and patina styling techniques.

Vinegar by itself is a mild acid, a food additive, an excellent cleaning agent, and a metal prep liquid. However, mix vinegar with a few otherwise inert materials, and it becomes an accelerant for oxidation on most metals.

nan-made and certainly influenced by more than nature.

Studying history also tells us that discoveries have been made regarding the patination of the ancient world. Egyptologists have discovered that chemicals were used to tint gold and other precious and semiprecious metals to simulate natural coloring on faces and clothing. Grecian and Roman statues show signs that ronze was also tinted to color and ecorate statues, even to make them eem older than they were. This hows us that manipulating the finsh of artwork has been acceptable and a standard in artwork and creativity through the ages.

There are some purists who reject he art of patination in automotive rt and restyling. Personally, I think hat if it is done properly it can yield a nostalgic and beautiful finish. The Statue of Liberty is a particularly iconic example of patina that is both beautiful and significant. The outer panels are made from 3/32 copper plate, which is about the thickness of two pennies stacked. It was delivered in the 1880s as a gift from the people of France to the people of the United States, symbolizing freedom and liberty.

The statue, designed by Frédéric-Auguste Bartholdi and constructed by architect Gustave Eiffel (known for designing the Eiffel Tower in France), was first erected as a polished copper statue. Recently, a restoration and refurbishment project has been performed that involved replacing some of the exterior, and the obvious challenge was to match the patina of the antique panels seamlessly to retain the historical significance and appearance of Lady Liberty. The restoration team's process was to apply mild acids to etch and degrade the surface and then use an accelerated chemical process to properly and seamlessly color match the new copper to the old. A mixture of African Violet liquid fertilizer and distilled water was used to accelerate the green pigment, which worked exceptionally well to blend the repaired and replaced panels in with the original copper panels.

Fauxtina in the Film Industry

The motion picture and television industries are in the business of making us believe that we've been transported to another time and place. This is precisely what adding

frican violet fertilizer is a soil acidifier. It's used in agriculture as a growth supplement for many plants and flowers, but can also be used to accelerate the patina development on certain metals, such as copper and brass. Several projects uring the Statue of Liberty restoration in 2012 used similar fertilizers to match the original patina of the copper plating n Lady Liberty.

The movie American Graffiti *has become legendary for its historical accuracy and period correctness in everything from cultural language trends to automotive styling and historical representation. This image is a tribute to Mel's Diner in the movie and is currently a pop culture display in Japan. Patina techniques were used in recreating this snapshot in time on both the vehicles and structures.*

patina to a vehicle is attempting to do, so there's much to learn from movies.

We judge a movie by how realistic the effects are. We've become accustomed to amazing special effects that are historically accurate down to the finest details. The bar is raised on what we observe not only in movies but also television programs that are dated to a specific time in history. The need for accuracy in historical storytelling goes back to the beginning of film itself. Continuity between period-correct housing and a specific year range of vehicles in a particular scene is critical; discern-

ing eyes will pick apart inaccuracies and disqualify a film based on first impressions alone, despite what the script, storyline, or even actors have to contribute to the work.

Creating the sense of suspended disbelief is the number-one priority of a filmmaker. Having the viewers immerse themselves into the experience instead of looking at the images before them is a necessity for a successful movie experience. These days, computer-generated imagery (CGI) plays a key role in the production of a film. Though it is a wonderful tool to recreate other worlds and times, a person still has to program the

scenes, create the styling, and mak us believe that a dinosaur can be i a chase scene with a Jeep at a them park or that a Camaro can twist an flip itself into a giant robot from far-off galaxy.

CGI is a sophisticated tool t create patina in a digital format. prop stylist has an important job i commercial film production doin set design and prop styling. A pro stylist can labor for days to cre ate a layer of dust that looks like i took a decade to settle. The digit manipulation and prop styling o three-dimensional pieces needs t be in perfect sync to blend togethe

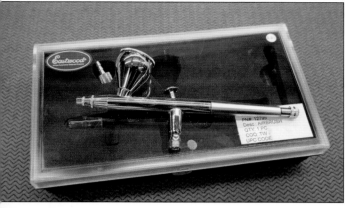

This dual-action airbrush opens up an entire new world of detail painting. Mastering the airbrush takes many years of practice, but a few basic techniques that are included in this book will give you the ability to create realistic patina within minutes of picking up the airbrush for the very first time!

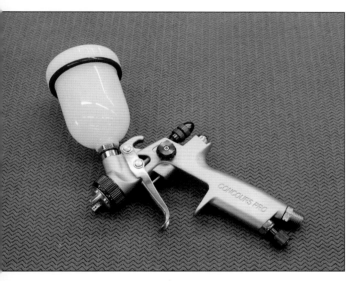

This is a detail gun that shares the same controls as a full-size pneumatic (air-driven) spray gun. The smaller size provides great control on medium to small projects and is versatile for many effects and painting methods.

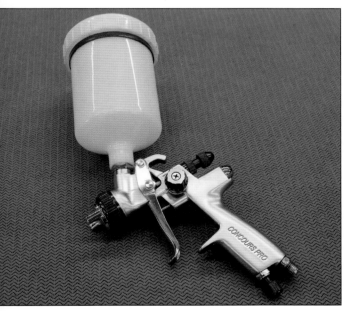

The full-size high-volume, low-pressure (HVLP) spray gun is the industry standard for automotive refinishing. These guns require some practice to use, but they are simple to set up for accurate paint delivery.

in a realistic format that viewers can agree to believing in, even if for a short time.

The professionals in the movie industry use specialized tools to create their illusions. The purpose of this book is to give you the tools to create the illusion that your vehicle, furniture, or artwork is older than it seems with accurate and realistic character.

Patina-Friendly Tools, Supplies, and Paints

Creativity and the willingness to experiment are probably the most important tools you can have when creating patina. Putting in the work to practice and experiment is critical, but there are some tools that will help make the job easier.

Pneumatic spray equipment is not necessary but will help you create aged effects on large surfaces, such as automotive panels. An airbrush and a high-volume, low-pressure (HVLP) gun are important tools for the projects in this book (see chapter 7 for airbrush specifics).

Disposable paint brushes called chip brushes are easy to use. Sometimes they lose hair (actually a good thing), and they leave a pronounced texture when used with automotive paint.

A paint roller designed for latex paint also gives a distinct texture to undercoats and topcoats, which can be used to create a blend of color and texture that mimics aging.

Automotive paint can be toxic and dangerous to use. However, there are some non-catalyzed paints, such as lacquers and enamels, out there that are less dangerous. Chemical compatibility is essential in the collision repair and automotive restoration worlds, but sometimes

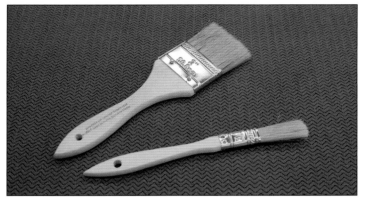

Chip brushes are inexpensive because they're not the best quality paintbrush. This makes them easy to abuse. I find them particularly effective in craft painting and dry-brushing techniques that create interesting effects while patina painting.

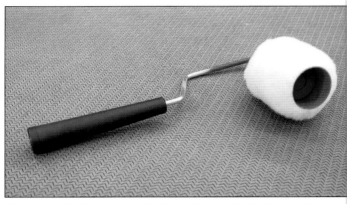

A paint roller is an excellent way to create texture in the base coat of a paint job or to mimic a rough and worn (or even poorly applied) vintage paint job. Don't be afraid to experiment with these tools! Creativity and fearlessness yield great results in the patina world.

a reaction between incompatible paints creates a desired effect of peeling or degraded paint when creating patina. While we hope that you are safely applying all paints, don't be afraid to experiment!

Setting Up the Paint Shop

One of the first considerations when starting a project is to decide where you are going to apply your patina. You're going to need some space. Cars are big, and you need to be able to walk freely around your subject in order to apply a finish to it. Even refinishing a few parts at a time takes plenty of room. Refinishing panels on stands, a disassembled motorcycle, or even an antique gas pump will require enough space to have access to every part of the piece.

It goes without saying that you'll need plenty of airflow in your shop. Solvents evacuating from wet paint as part of the drying and curing process will need to be removed from the space, and good airflow is necessary for drying. Fumes from automotive paint are hazardous and need to be respected. Adequate airflow needs to

We realize not everyone has a professional paint booth in the backyard. All of the projects, demonstrations, and samples in this book have been prepared in our own studio garage so you have a realistic idea of what is possible in a home shop environment.

Although this is not the optimum air supply, a storage tank can be a solution. It may work for small projects where a spray gun is used or for a large airbrush project that uses a pressure regulator to control airflow.

Common furnace filters create a well-ventilated shop area. We taped filters in place on the floor and door to facilitate a cross breeze and to clear the air of any fumes or overspray during the painting process.

e established no matter what your painting environment. Sometimes creating airflow is as simple as opening a window and cracking open a garage door. If you have the luxury of using a formal paint booth, these needs will definitely be met. You'll need to assess your situation and create a path for air to escape to maintain a safe work area.

If your painting or prep area is a converted garage, you'll want to protect other items inside it. Sanding dust is very fine and will quickly form a silty layer on your tools, workbenches, and anything else that's stored in the garage. As you are planning your materials list and budgets, add in the cost for drop cloths, masking tape, and cleaning supplies to not only prepare for the upcoming mess but to clean up afterward as well.

If you are wet sanding, you will have the runoff from your vehicle to consider. Wet sanding residue can eventually drain into the local water table if it gets washed into a storm drain, so do your best to eliminate potential pollution while painting your project.

If your work area is an attached garage, be aware that paint fumes can be quite annoying if they leach into your home. Overspray can also drift and find its way through door gaps and window frames. These things can cause irritation to people who are not wearing proper safety equipment.

Carefully consider your paint environment to make sure that you're not going to have any surprises down the road. Above all, make sure that you're being safe and that you're considering the safety of those around you.

Pneumatic Tools

To do a complete paint automotive job you need a compressor that will keep up with your demand. This usually means at least a 5-hp pump, a 60-gallon air storage tank, and preferably a two-stage motor that

Industrial applications demand enormous air delivery. This 65-cfm screw-type compressor is overkill for our patina projects and for most paint jobs, but it provides large volumes of CFM for our other needs, such as fresh breathable air or sandblasting jobs.

delivers at least 13 to 15 cfm at a reasonable pressure. When I'm coaching hobbyists, I often hear, "I have a 20-gallon tank on my 3-hp compressor. Can I still paint a full-size truck with it?" My answer is always: "Yes, but you shouldn't."

A small compressor on a big job makes the pump work too hard, creating nothing but hot air filled with moisture that will eventually end up in your work. It's always best to have too much air supply, which minimizes the moisture in the lines and supply chain so that it can be filtered out before it ends up in your paint. Mistakes are part of the equation of some patina paint jobs, but it's always best to have as much control over your equipment as possible so that you can choose where your defects are.

Although a pumpless air tank is not going to get you very far on a large paint job, it will work for small parts with a detail gun. A pumpless air tank will give you several hours of air if you're using an airbrush. The size of your patina project will determine if you need to invest in compressor equipment.

The other end of the spectrum is a massive 65-cfm screw-type air compressor that is mounted to a 120-gallon air tank. This machine can run nonstop. Since it has an integrated air-cooling system, it can handle all but the most-demanding projects. The average full-size spray gun only needs 10 to 13 cfm, so this size could easily support five painters spraying around the clock.

Safety

Automotive paint is hazardous to use! Paints with catalysts (hardeners) are toxic and dangerous, even when they're dry. Urethane catalysts remain active for 90 days during the cure process, so even sanding dust can be toxic shortly after paint products have been applied. There are a few things you can do to protect yourself:

- Wear gloves whenever handling paint.
- Wear safety glasses at all times.
- Wear proper respiratory equipment . . . you only have one set of lungs so protect yourself!
- Wear protective clothing to keep

paint and fumes from getting trapped in your clothing.

Most automotive paints must b disposed of properly and safely, so b

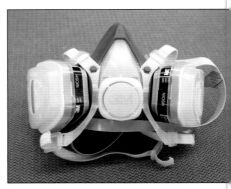

This is a charcoal filter spray mask approved by the National Institute for Occupational Safety and Health (NIOSH). It is capable of filtering out hazardous organic and industrial contamination as long as it's used within its shelf life. Do your homewor on whatever paint system you're usin to make sure you're protecting your respiratory system properly.

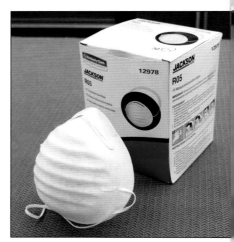

Even during simple duties, such as sanding or cleaning up, it's a good idea to use dust masks to keep your respiratory system protected. These are inexpensive and easy to use. I highly recommend keeping a box of these within reach on any automotive paint project.

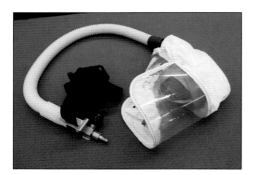

The best protection for applying automotive paint is with a fresh air–supplied system. This hood supplies the painter with breathable air from a dedicated air source and is the safest way to apply hazardous paint systems.

Nitrile gloves will protect your hands from most materials and will certainly keep your skin contaminants (oils and acids) off of your paint projects. They're an inexpensive way to help control your work environment and health.

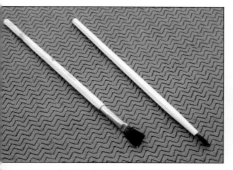

These model-building brushes came from a hobby store nearly 20 years ago. When properly cleaned, they will come in handy with patina painting in many ways.

Crackle paints are mostly used for furniture projects, but they are a fun way to create the illusion of an aged surface. Experiment with craft styling paints like this. You never know what effects you can recreate.

For the final detailing of our main project, this product was a great tool. The primer contains iron that will eventually rust on its own, but the accelerator/activator created rust in minutes.

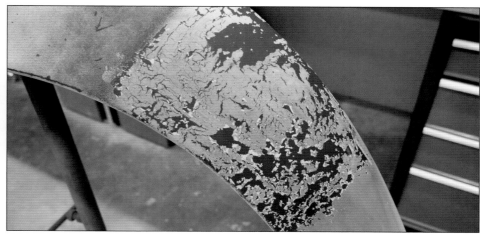

This is a combination of acrylic paints, crackle paint, and automotive paint. It was a little too drastic for our projects, but it was definitely fun to mess around with!

aware of the laws in your area. Find out how to safely dispose of paint in a responsible manner. Most communities have a hazardous disposal day at least once a year when you can turn in hazardous waste for a small fee, or sometimes for free, at the local landfill or convenience center. Do your research before you start your project so that you know what your local bylaws are for proper and legal hazardous materials disposal.

Craft Paints and Supplies

Products from the hobby industry can be used quite successfully when painting patina. The DIY craft industry has exploded in recent years, and there are many wonderful products available to create effects that simulate aged furniture, jewelry, or other items. There are rusting primers, crackled and distressed furniture kits, as well as online tutorials that show homemade methods for creating patina. Don't be afraid to go outside the automotive toybox for ideas!

Professional tools are not always needed, and unconventional thinking is a huge benefit. A grasp of cer-

tain automotive refinishing concepts is also helpful, but it's not required. The paints and techniques in this book are easy to use, and a first-time painter can get excellent results by following along.

Experimenting is probably one of the high points of creating fauxtina, and it can be a very fun process. I found it incredibly rewarding when I cracked the code on how to recreate bubbling rust on a car panel. It's one thing to find a rusted-out fender, but quite another to be able to create the look of a rusted fender and have complete control over the stage, style, color, and extent of your patina! The best thing about this book is that I can pass on step-by-step instructions, so you can create patina on your own terms.

Patina painting has been around for thousands of years, and it has been a trend in the automotive painting and restoration world for many years as well. Whether your reasons for doing a fauxtina paint job are personal, professional, or budget-oriented, I hope you have fun learning how to outsmart time and to lock in your version of automotive history!

FINDING YOUR LIGHT!

Sunlight brings with it much of what is needed to deteriorate any surface over time: ultraviolet energy. Man-made surfaces, particularly painted surfaces, are susceptible to UV damage that manifests in what we refer to as patina. This energy from the sun gives us a clue and great direction as to how to emulate organic patina.

Everything exposed to our atmosphere is subject to chemical changes and breakdown. Metals rust and plastics deteriorate, and paint is no different. In order to understand how paint deteriorates, we need to know a little about its history as well as its chemistry.

History and Chemistry

Paint systems break down on a molecular level and oxygenate (a $3 word for fade). What actually happens is a layer is formed between the paint film and the atmosphere, covering up the paint and changing its appearance. Different paint chemistry has different reactions to atmosphere: older paint systems that have more heavy metals, different resins and binders, and less film thickness will show fading differently than a modern basecoat clearcoat system.

The Studebaker Brothers Manufacturing Company in South Bend, Indiana, used to advertise with pride that the process of painting a carriage took 52 days to complete. This was due to the steps of applying, sanding, and reapplying paint, allowing ample dry time for the finish to be as beautiful as it was strong. Then in 1921, nitrocellulose lacquer was accidentally invented. This invention (or discovery, depending on how you look at history) gave paint enough viscosity to withstand spray application, revolutionizing the way a paint finish is applied. A 1924 Pontiac was the first car that was spray-painted.

Compared to today's paint finishes, the lacquer systems of the 1920s and 1930s were very weak. But coatings became stronger as innovations were introduced. During World War II, European paint manufacturers were restricted as to what chemicals they could use for coatings. They had to steer away from cotton-derived paints, such as nitrocellulose paints, due to the limited availability of cotton. Instead, they focused on plastic- and petroleum-based technology, which eventually became standard due to its superior strength and durability. To this day, the United States is

led by European innovation in pair technology.

In the 1930s, most vehicles wer painted with simple colors that wer rather dull compared to today's pa ate. Colors tended to be drab an similar to some primers, whic explains why there is not a big cor trast between the color itself and th rusted panel where paint has fade and worn through.

Metallic specialty colors starte appearing on cars in the 1930: The sparkly paint was first derive from fish scales that were mixe into pigment and resin bases. Thes paints and colors were not seen o mass-produced vehicles because the were very expensive to create an apply. They were only applied t upscale automobiles.

A less-expensive option wa brought into mainstream automc tive production in the early 1950 by Alcoa Aluminum. It produce the metallic effect by adding alumi num flakes to paint colors, whic is still an effect additive in today paint systems. Aluminum oxid plastic media, and other brigh additives intermix with the resi as you build the layers of the pain job, giving dimension that wouldn

his is the original and faded paint on the hood of a 2000 150 truck. The gloss is completely gone, and the clear- oat has deteriorated to the point that it is flaking off in ultiple places. An easy way to tell if it's a clearcoat paint b is if the oxidation is white, regardless of the base color.

This is an example of a non-factory finish that is delam- inating. The clear is still "clear" for the most part, but it is clearly separating from the base color. Once this hap- pens, there's no saving the paint. To repair it, it has to be stripped to the primer or bare substrate and redone.

is 1964 Ford was abandoned for decades, as the ate of deterioration and original and horribly neglected ngle-stage paint finish shows. This was originally a bright d color, but it has turned to a hazy dark orange that can ver be brought back to its former gloss. Notice that it des within the range of color it started as and **does not** idize white as a clearcoat finish will.

Here's another great example of patina to emulate. The original paint has faded to the point of revealing the substrate to the elements and atmosphere. Despite the rusty appearance, this is still mild surface rust that hides a relatively solid panel under the oxidation. The flaking paint under the trim is interesting, and the rust streaks that run down into the white are authentic. This Studebaker is complete with many valuable parts, including the acrylic ornaments on the fender peaks.

This 1937 Ford sports an updated interior and drivetrain but completely original paint and trim. Wear and deterioration of the paint are extreme, but the underlying sheet metal doesn't seem to have been affected much.

It's difficult to see the blue topcoat color that once covered the black undercoat on this 1951 Ford. The light blue metallic paint has been photochemically stripped off of th[e] top surfaces, revealing the undercoat and the bare sheet metal of the fender.

Metallics, such as this one from a mid-1960s Buick, have aluminum flakes and pigment mixed into the resin base. Aluminum oxidizes very quickly once exposed to damaging UV rays, and it can overtake the pigment, as it's done here, giving the blue color a very silvery appearance.

The 1940s showed us a lot mo[re] chrome and stainless steel trim, [as] well as single-colored cars. In th[e] 1950s, mass-produced vehicles use[d] aluminum-infused topcoat co[l]ors that had a more subtle metall[ic] appearance. The metallic particl[es] compromised the color strength an[d] made these colors particularly su[s]ceptible to UV damage.

The cars of the 1970s featured [a] lot of earth tones, dark gold, bronz[e,] and brown. For several years in th[e] mid 1990s, a high percentage of ne[w] vehicles were produced in green co[l]ors. In 2015, dark brown made a hug[e] comeback with manufacturers, pa[r]ticularly import carmakers. As pai[nt] technology continued to progres[s,] so has the depth and complexity [of] paint colors.

Oxidation

New paint has a distinctly clea[n] look to it; it is glossy and has a sha[rp] distinctness of image (DOI), whic[h] is a statement on the quality [of] the reflection. For example, a gla[ss]

otherwise be possible in a solid color. Decades-old metallic paint becomes rather chalky looking and uneven. It is challenging to replicate this look into fauxtina, but if done correctly, it can be a great effect.

Automotive paint color trends come and go in phases that are sometimes driven by technology and sometimes driven by social and cultural swings. Often, auto manufacturers create new colors and styles in anticipation of a color trend catching on and becoming popular. In the 1920s, some vehicle manufacturers created vivid paint jobs. Using lively primary colors defied the depression era by showing an attractive, shiny vehicle that ignored the socioeconomic effects of the Great Depression. Bright colors were a clever marketing strategy, but it was not intended for the majority of mass-produced vehicles.

This 1934 Packard represents a time in America when money was scarce and cars like this were very expensive. Vivid colors were sometimes chosen as a marketing tool to lift the spirits of consumers, and they were an incentive to discriminating buyers.

We obviously have a rusty truck that is slowly being reclaimed by nature. The paint color and the rusted metal are very similar, so is the paint rusty? In a sense, yes, it is. When you break down exactly what rust is and how similar the fading process is to the rusting process, it's pretty safe to say that, in fact, paint rusts.

The DOI on this newly painted Jaguar is outstanding. This clearcoated finish has been sanded, leveled, and polished back to a mirror gloss. You can see by the crisp reflections of the lights and details in the paint that a lot of time and effort was spent perfecting this paint job.

This early 1960s F150 shows neglected paint with no DOI at all. In fact, it actually looks like primer. Believe it or not, this paint can be brought back to somewhat of a shine. Due to the UV damage from years of exposure and neglect, it will never have its original shine and the strength of the paint itself is lost forever. Even after polishing and waxing, it will soon lose its gloss again.

mirror has a nearly perfect DOI, whereas most new-car paint jobs have an orange-peel look to the surface that gives a slightly distorted reflection. Aged paint typically has a poor DOI because of the oxidation that occurs on the surface.

Oxidation is a chemical reaction between the surface and the atmosphere. This creates a layer, or an opaque filter, between the color and the observer. The oxidized layer can be removed using polishing techniques and rubbing compounds that have fine abrasives embedded in them, which can bring the paint back to a high gloss most of the time.

Oxidation on paint is a close cousin to conventional rust, though it is different from the degraded iron oxide that happens with metal. The two processes are so close on a molecular chemical level that I always say that any substrate can rust! Air pollution is another factor in how paint and other surfaces degrade over time. If there's a lot of a sulfide in the air due to industrial fallout, painted surfaces don't last as long. It's just an easy way of saying that surfaces degrade over time with UV and atmospheric exposure.

Think of oxidation as rust. Realizing that there are sometimes different layers of oxidation that react differently over time can help you recreate, accelerate, and mimic the effects of aging on paint. Solid, single-stage colors react much differently than clearcoated colors. Creating patina is essentially visualizing what nature does to certain coatings and colors and reverse engineering the process. The quality of the fauxtina is dependent on the research and execution of the artist doing the project.

How Paint Ages

Everyone knows that paint fades. Bright colors become muted, reds turn orangey, blues become lighter,

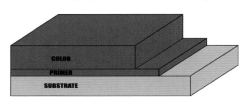

Most cars from the 1930s to late 1970s had a single-stage paint job applied at the manufacturer. This shows you the layers of color and gloss that were engineered into one layer of paint. It's easy to visualize how this can quickly deteriorate and fade, if not wear down to the primer layers with exposure to the atmosphere, pollution, and UV damage from the sun.

and white typically yellows, But why? There's more than one influence that makes paint fade. The chalkiness of old single-stage paint is typically due to UV exposure, but pollution and other chemicals in the atmosphere play a part as well. The powdery film that collects on older nonclearcoated paints can contain some of the pigment from the underlying paint, thereby giving it a slightly lighter color than the original paint.

Automotive manufacturers began using two-stage paint systems during vehicle construction in the mid 1980s. They phased two-stage paint in as the main refinish system through the 1990s. Clearcoated paints take on very different characteristics when aged and degraded.

Since the clearcoat is designed as a UV barrier to the pigment, it typically keeps the chalky oxidation from forming. It does a better job of filtering the harmful UV rays that will also fade color. While the vivid colors may fade under the clearcoat, the clear layer will last much longer.

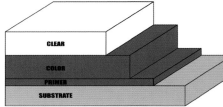

This cross-section represents a modern finish with a layer of clearcoat over the base color. Since the top layer is very strong and chemical resistant, the color will last longer, even when the clearcoat itself begins to degrade and lose gloss. However, once the clear layer loses strength and allows UV rays to deteriorate the color layer through the weakened clearcoat, the two layers can separate, causing delamination and peeling of the clear layer.

The top of the door frame gets more sun, which causes more of a chance of weakening and eventually peeling of clearcoat. Delamination of the clearcoat on an upper surface can be seen on this panel.

efore it finally breaks down. Once t degrades, the clearcoat will allow xidation *under* the surface layer of learcoat, creating a whitening and ubbling effect that is quite unatractive. Degraded clearcoat turns nilky white and begins to delamiate from the layer of color.

The actual color of the paint can ive a clue as to where the pigment s going to shift. A color wheel is a niversal representation of the specrum of colors in the prism and how hey transition from one to another. Vithin the color wheel are the three rimary colors: blue, red, and yelow. All other colors are derived of

shades of these three primary colors. You can look at a color wheel and see what direction a color takes on in relation to the three primary colors.

An easy way to remember all of the color tones in the spectrum of light is to memorize the acronym ROYGBIV (Roy-Gee-Biv). It is the first letters of red, orange, yellow, green, blue, indigo, and violet. It's important to know these colors and the order in which they appear in the spectrum of light. The order of ROYGBIV provides clues to color direction, color fading, and especially color tinting. So, know it! Learn it! Love it!

The other element of a color wheel that is important to know is that the value, or intensity, of the color is lighter on the inside of this color wheel. This gives us another tool to determine what a faded color might look like as it gets older. Since

we know that faded paint is lighter, we can use the color wheel to figure out what is an authentic color direction as well as an authentic value (intensity) to give the illusion of naturally faded paint.

For instance, turquoise is between green and blue but not quite yellow on the color wheel. That shows you the direction of the color from either of the primary colors that it is closest to (blue or yellow). Turquoise has a lot more green than yellow in it, so the color will most likely fade to green instead of yellow. The color will also be more green than blue, even though blue is strong in the blend of pigments. Add in a layer of chalky oxidation, and the chalk film diminishes the gloss and filters the color, creating a combination effect. Orange is between red and yellow. The tone of that orange will give you a clue as to whether it's a reddish or dark orange or a yellower orange.

Using the Sun

There is one simple rule that will guide you in creating authentic patina regardless of your color or vehicle choice: Paint fades from the top down. Simply put, there will be more damage on the top surfaces of a vehicle regardless of the style, color, or chemistry of a given paint finish.

In general, all things exposed to the sun and UV rays degrade from the top down. The shingles on your roof get lighter, stained wood on handrails gets faded faster than the spindles under them, and even fruit ripens and colors differently at the tops of trees. The sugar content in cherries is much higher at the upper third of the tree than at the bottom, which is a direct result of being exposed to more sunlight.

A color wheel is a valuable tool. It can show you how a color may fade and what to add to strengthen them or make them more vivid.

The paint on this Chrysler fades from green to grey to red oxide. The upper exposed edges are recipients of most of the UV damage.

This truck has obvious color deterioration on the top of the fender. The flat part of the hood shares the same fate, but the vertical surfaces kept the color intact.

Horizontal surfaces also fade faster than vertical surfaces. So, the hood fades faster than the doors.

This rule provides an excellent starting point for designing the faux-tina for your project. It can help you look for the most accurate original color, and it will give you a range of patina examples to emulate.

Creating Character

If you're not sure about the history of your vehicle, you can use your imagination and create possible scenarios that might explain the patina: Is it a barn find? Is it an abandoned vehicle found in the Arizona desert? Both of those conditions have a very specific type and severity of patina that you can recreate with some research and practice.

Studying how patina is different in specific geographies and conditions is important. It will give you the tools to carefully and authentically create a great conversation piece, a paint job that is a ton of fun to create, and a vehicle that you will be proud to display.

The hood on this truck is mostly faded to metal, but it's uneven from side to side. This can be for a number of reasons. One reason could be that perhaps the truck was sitting partially covered.

PRACTICE MAKES PERFECT

Perfecting your paint technique by practicing will give you the confidence you need to do an excellent job, regardless of your goals. Even hobby painters make a regular practice out of doing "spray outs" on separate test panels to get a feel for gun settings, color selection, and temperature recommendations, as well as to improve muscle memory.

You need to have a strategy to be comfortable moving into your paint job to achieve the patina of your choice. When you look closely at a worn paint job, you'll notice that there are several different aged effects that need to be recreated, depending on the area. There can be wear around the driver door, sun damage on the top panels, delamination and rust on lower sections, and abrasive damage and rock chips on the leading edge of some panels.

Aged Effects

A realistic patina job becomes much easier if you break it down into specific sections. We will focus on the main types of patina: wear damage, sun damage, and impact damage. Mimicking these effects takes some consideration, so let's break it down to three categories.

Wear Damage

One thing to remember is a paint layer is very thin. Most factory paint jobs are only 2.5 mm total thickness, so it stands to reason that the paint can wear through in certain places over time. Certain areas are more susceptible to wear, such as the door handles, scuff plates and rocker panels, the bottom of the door glass opening where someone's arm may hang over, and even the edges of a hood where it may have been handled opening and closing for decades.

Another common spot to find wear damage is around the ignition key. Wear to a factory single-stage metallic paint job can create an interesting pattern under the bezel. Wear damage can also create a matte finish

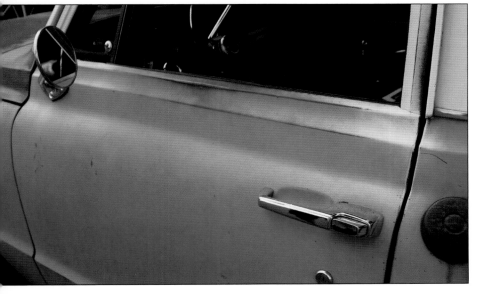

This late 1960s pickup shows its great natural patina with much of the original color still on the panel. The wear occurs naturally where a driver's arm would hang out the window. This vehicle doesn't have an air conditioner, so driving with the window down and using the opening as an armrest would be common.

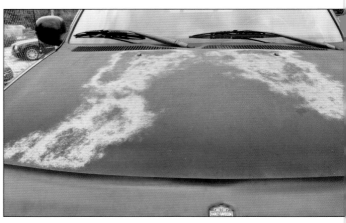

A keychain swinging from the dash for 50 years created a distinctive pattern on the paint of this 1966 C10 truck. This is original and very subtle. Sometimes one can accentuate wear like this in the spirit of creating an effect and still maintain realism in the patina.

This 2000 F150 has a badly damaged clearcoat finish. As clearcoat degrades, it turns lighter and becomes chalky white before it completely delaminates. This wear is from the sunlight and UV energy oxidizing the color under the clear, causing it to separate.

on a vehicle that was once semigloss. This occurs because as the color is worn away so are the resins that hold the gloss.

Vehicles that have natural patina and worn paint provide clues as to the history of the vehicle. They also give inspiration for age effects to recreate on paint.

Sun Damage

The combination of time and exposure to sunshine and the elements is damaging to paint coatings, plastics, and rubber. Most of the time, it results in lightening of the colors, loss of glossiness, flaking, and deterioration. The degree of that damage and how it looks is what we are calling patina, but sometimes it is simply referred to as faded paint.

Newer clearcoat paint jobs show sun damage much differently than a single-stage enamel or lacquer paint job from the 1950s or 1960s. Due to the two stages of a clearcoat, the clear typically degrades first. It turns whitish and then flakes off and exposes the underlying color. The color then fades and allows moisture penetra-

tion to the metal, eventually causing rust to show.

With single-stage paint, the fading layers of paint do not take on the whiteish appearance like a clearcoat. Instead, the layers stay a relatively similar color to the topcoat. Looking at the center of a badly faded panel, you can typically see the undercoat colors that are revealed as the topcoat

color oxidizes away. This is much mo[re] pleasing to look at (in my opinio[n] and certainly much easier to replicat[e]

For the most part, this boo[k] will focus on replicating patina [on] single-stage (direct gloss, direct colo[r]) paint. This is simply because it rep[-] resents similar technology that wa[s] used in the 1920s through 1960s o[n] mass-produced vehicles.

The roof panel on this 1960s car with a single-stage off-white color is much more damaged than the rest of the body. It is the largest panel on the car and is lopsided in its fading. Many different factors can cause this, but it's quite common that panels wear in an uneven manner.

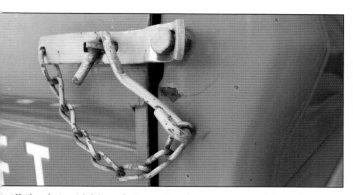

ntil the late 1960s, vintage trucks were considered trac-
rs with doors. Many of the mechanisms were quite crude
ntil the trucks were finally recognized as passenger vehi-
es as well as work vehicles. Case in point, the tailgate
tches were a stud, a swing latch with a hook, a loop on
e tailgate, and a chain to keep everything from dropping
to the mud. That's not much different from the gate latch
n a covered wagon! The chain on this truck has left a wit-
ess mark on the paint, and the latch has made an arched
ear pattern under the main stud on the bed.

The leading edge of any vehicle takes the brunt of most of
the damage, whether it's sun damage, rock chips, or rubbing up against objects during the life of the vehicle. Here
the headlight housing is showing deep chips, scratches,
and exposed metal that are all beginning at the front and
lessening at the back.

Impact Damage

There is a type of paint dam-
ge that is not caused by natural or
hemical elements. For example, a
ilgate chain on a vintage pickup
an cause a distinctive wear mark or
itness mark as it comes into con-
ct with the paint repeatedly over
me. Rock chips, damage to leading
dges of panels and rocker panels,
nd even collision damage all have
stinctive signatures that can be
created.

The leading edge of vehicles such
fender peaks, hood lips, and bum-
ers sustain damage from rocks and
her objects hitting the front of
e panel during decades of use and
use. The variety of the composition
the panels (some being pot-metal,
me chrome) may mean that there
no visible rust showing through
e paint. Keep this in mind when
creating natural-looking wear from
pact damage, and know how your
aterials react to atmosphere. The
al is to find what happens organ-

ically and recreate it with a subtle
effect that looks realistic.

Undercoats and Primer Colors

Undercoats are different colors on different types of vehicles.
Vehicle manufacturers determine
what coating lies under the visible
topcoats based on several reasons.
Certain vintage paint jobs have red
oxide primers, some have black,
and some have neutral grey. Red
oxide was very common in Chevrolet vehicles of the 1950s and 1960s.
Black primer seemed to be common
in Dodge, Plymouth, and Chrysler
vehicles. Many older vehicles have
been poorly refinished or have had
panels that have been repaired badly,
and this can reveal different colored
primers and different layers of paint.

Modern auto manufacturers
use color-keyed sealers and primers to minimize the amount of topcoat that needs to be applied. These

undercoats are almost exactly the
same color as the topcoat, so only a
minimal amount needs to be applied
for color effect and match (saving
cost on manufacturing). As an added
bonus, the damage isn't as noticeable
from a distance in the event of road
damage, rock chips, or even deep
scratches.

Creating your own patina allows
you to choose the undercoat color,
giving you the option to color coordinate the effect and look that you
want on your project. This is one of
the benefits of "patinizing" your own
vehicle: you can match interior colors, wheels, or a specific time period
that you have an affinity to.

Test Panels

I *always* advocate practicing different types of effects on a panel
before committing to the project,
regardless of the nature of the refinish job. You can fine-tune the style
and designs you want to create with

You need to protect yourself while handling sharp metal and any paint materials. Nitrile gloves will protect your skin from paint exposure and keep your skin's oils and acids off of your project. A protective mask and a well-ventilated area are a must for spraying paint.

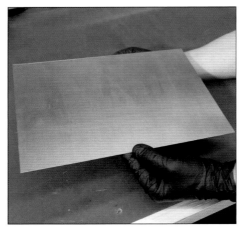

We found our metal at a home center for a few dollars for all three panels. You can use any substrate for these test panels, but we suggest using something similar to your project. In our case, that meant using thin sheet metal.

some simple primers and paints fo our test panels. You'll need som inexpensive light gauge metal tha similar to automotive sheet meta We suggest 22-gauge metal becau it is inexpensive and available at se eral different stores. You'll also nee some scuffing pads to prep the met to ensure adhesion of the prim and paint, as well as some 400- ar 600-grit wet or dry sandpaper.

We are creating three test panel one for each of the types of damag (wear, sun, and impact). Each pan is prepared exactly the same so w can understand clearly how to cr ate three distinctly different patina This will also give you a good id of how different prep techniqu with the same materials will sim late patina. This exercise is designe for you to become comfortable wit sanding and exposing the underl ing layers of paint and using the co trasting colors to mimic paint th has deteriorated from the top to th ground coats.

The type of paint is less important than the color strategy. That said, we'll be using mostly solvent-based paints due the increased durability and similarity to what was used when the vehicle was manufactured. We're using a black aerosol for the ground coat, a red oxide primer for the middle layer, and a pale yellow for the topcoat.

Prepping the Panels

Start by scuffing your panels wit sandpaper or a scuffing pad. Use fir pressure and be thorough, but don try to do anything but scratch th outer surface. It is necessary for th surface to be abraded before pai application because this gives th paint something to hang on to. Th scuffing can be a fast process, depen ing on what your substrate is. It too three to five minutes on our panels

Follow by cleaning your met panels with a solvent-based cleane These cleaners are available in aer sol form or as liquid in pourab containers. If you don't have an body shop products handy, aceton or naphtha from a home center wi work well.

much less stress on a test panel. Plus, mistakes are easier to recover from on a small fender or panel! You can end up with some cool souvenirs of your project as well. Make practice panels a part of your project for no other reason than to understand how to create different patina effects.

I know many custom painters who do spray-out panels for their

customers long before they begin the final paint on the project. They use the panels to confirm they are on the same page as the customer as well as develop the technique they will use for the actual vehicle.

You can create practice panels and hone your patina-making skills along with us. We're using metal sourced from a home center and

Scuffing the Panels

To have proper adhesion, you must sand the metal panel to create a mechanical bond. A red scuffing [pa]d and some elbow grease (pressure) will create enough [too]th on the panel for the first layers of paint to stick well. [Th]e rest of our colors will bond into the first color coat.

2 After scuffing, precleaning is necessary. Solvent cleaners are available at body shop supply stores, but there are alternatives if you don't have one around. Home centers and hardware stores have a variety of chemicals that will act as a solvent cleaner. By the way, make sure you're wearing gloves for these preparation steps! Solvents can be absorbed into your bloodstream very quickly through your skin.

3 While the solvent is still wet, wipe it all the way off the panel in one direction. This makes sure you're not just smearing around contamination. Allow the panel to dry for 5 to 10 minutes after wiping the solvent off and before painting.

Our ground coat is black, which mimics a lot of vehicle manufacturers' metal sealers and base primers. Each layer of undercoat must have at least three wet coats in order to layer enough material to tolerate sanding some of it off and still showing color.

The red oxide primer is a nice contrast to the black. It easily shows when the black layer is completely covered. Apply at least four coats of red oxide, waiting 5 to 10 minutes or until the gloss has gone from the coat. The red oxide will mimic the undercoat that many vehicles had directly under the topcoat color.

Once your primer is on the panel, let sit at least 30 minutes before applying your topcoat. This wait time will allow solvents to evacuate from the layers and will ensure that your topcoat col will have enough of a barrier so it doesn't lift and wrinkle the underlying primer layers.

We happened to like the pale yellow color we're using, but the choice is yours. When you are creating a test panel for a specific project, it is a good idea to match the color to your project to get an even clearer idea of how it will actually look on your car. It took us one full coat plus another light coat for complete coverage. Use no more topcoat than is necessary!

Painting the Panels

For our color strategy, we'll use black ground coat, a red oxide prime and a pale yellow finish coat on ea panel. Spray three wet coats of t black primer on each of the cle and sanded metal samples. Wait fo to 10 minutes between coats.

Once all three coats are applie wait for at least 15 minutes befo moving on to your next lay which is primer. Apply four coats the red oxide primer. Waiting for to 10 minutes between coats on again.

After the primer coats are applie wait at least 30 minutes before spra ing the topcoat. Apply only enoug of your chosen topcoat color to hi the red primer. Our goal is to "fad through the top layer quickly a carefully expose the underlyi primer colors. We are using a yello topcoat for these test panels, and took one full coat and one very lig coat to get full coverage.

Spraying the Paint

When spraying paint, use a side-to-side motion, work from the bottom to the top, and overlap each pass 50 percent with another pass. This creates a very smooth layer of paint that is very even. Think of paint mimicking the layers of shingles on your house: they're laid halfway over each other and eventually create a smooth and even covering on your roof. Your goal is the same with painting. The 50-percent overlap application technique is an industry standard regardless of the style or type of painting. ■

Practicing Patina Three Ways

Our goal is to imitate the three types of patina that were discussed at the beginning of this chapter: wear damage, sun damage, and impact damage. There are different strategies for all three, but all techniques involve using sandpaper to remove layers of color to expose what's underneath. We will practice all three techniques, and then you can decide which works best for your patina job.

Wear Damage

There are many areas on a vehicle that are prone to something rubbing on the paint. Door handles, fuel fillers, window openings, and scuff plates are all areas that get used and abused repeatedly. For this practice panel, we will create a faux window handle location. This area often had someone's hands, clothing, or knuckles rubbing the paint for years, slowly wearing through the finish. Our goal is to practice creating realistic wear under the handle.

Creating Wear Damage

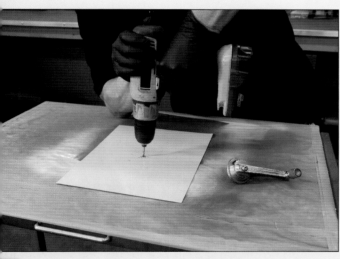

To give ourselves a realistic scenario, we placed a vintage window crank handle on our sample so we could simulate wear around it. We started with a pilot hole through the panel using a 1/8-inch drill bit.

2 Use a 5/16-inch bit to widen the pilot hole and allow for a screw to be inserted through the handle and panel.

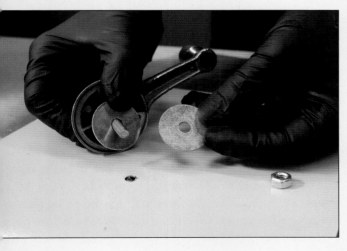

3 Place a flat washer on either side of the panel to steady the handle and simulate how it feels on the door trim inside the 1966 C10 truck it came from. If you don't have similar hardware lying around from older builds like we do, you can buy an inexpensive handle from a home center.

Creating Wear Damage *continued*

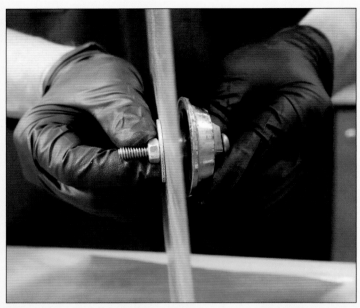

4 This angle shows exactly how the mock-up works on our panel. The nut is finger tight on the machine screw that goes through the handle.

5 Using a Stabilo or grease pencil (you can find thes at hobby stores or online art supply stores), trace the arc of travel as the window crank moves on its pivot point. This is now our temporary guide for creating wear damage on our sample panel.

6 Remove the handle and begin sanding with 400-grit wet/dry sandpaper to expose the undercoats. The 400-grit sandpaper is fairly aggressive with the relatively thin coats of aerosol paint, but it will still produce a fine enough scratch to appear as a faded line as we sand.

7 Lubricate the sandpaper as you sand. Fill a spray bottle with tap water and add a few drops of dishwashing liquid. Dishwashing liquid, such as Ajax or Palmolive, without moisturizers is preferred so no deposi are left on the panel. The added soap lubricates the pape and helps keep the grit from becoming clogged with pain

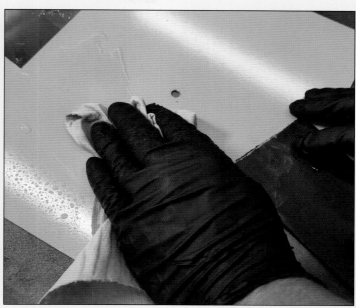

8 *The pencil mark will wear away quickly, but you'll get the idea of recreating the arc of the handle soon. Use a fingertip to focus the sandpaper and sand a narrow path.*

9 *After a dozen or so strokes, wipe the water and dust from the panel and check your progress. You want to carefully expose the layers, not dig holes!*

10 *You will start to notice the yellow giving way to the red oxide here. Have patience and carefully monitor sanding from this point.*

11 *Another 10 or 15 strokes reveal even more red oxide color. We are going for drastic wear on our panel, but the effect is up to you and what your goals are. Practice panels are made for experimenting, so you can be excessive just to see what happens.*

Creating Wear Damage *continued*

12 *Once you are satisfied with your wear, wipe away the sanding water and sludge. It is time for the next step.*

13 *Use 400-grit sandpaper to sand the entire panel, exposing grains of the undercoats all over. This makes the entire panel appear aged, not just around the handle, and creates a more realistic patina.*

14 *Sand the entire panel to reveal small flecks of color and a slightly faded look overall. Imperfections in the underlying layers enhance this effect and give the illusion of age.*

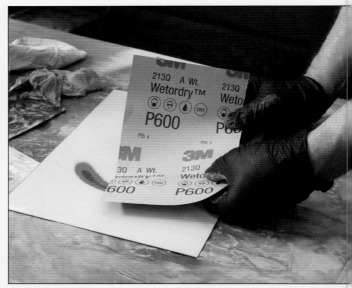

15 *Switch to 600-grit sandpaper to smooth the transitions between colors and give a more natural fade between layers. The 600-grit paper also eliminates any 400-grit scratches that look like sanding marks. We are going for a realistic-looking fade that happens from years of exposure and wear.*

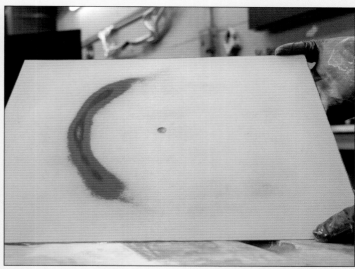

6 Sand the entire panel with 600-grit paper, being careful not to oversand the arc of wear under the andle. This will complete the subtle faded look on this ractice panel.

17 You can see the wear marks clearly, but what's also interesting is the yellow color fades in and out of tone. Some areas are bright, while some are milky looking. If you want more drastic fades, simply sand more. If you want a subtler effect, simply sand less and perhaps start with 600-grit paper.

8 Reinstall the handle on the machine screw to see the finished wear pattern as it would appear on a ehicle.

19 Thread the nut on the backside so the handle can be put into use. Test the arc to see if it matches the travel of the handle.

Creating Wear Damage continued

20 My worn zone closely matches the arc of the handle as it swings around and my knuckles rub exactly where the paint is the most worn down.

21 The finished product looks surprisingly authentic. More importantly, it gave us the opportunity for a trial run on creating this type of paint wear.

n Damage

To simulate many years of des-t sun damage, use the same grits of ndpaper (400 and 600 grit) but with an interface sanding pad and slightly different sanding techniques. Our goal here is to create the look of an upper horizontal panel, such as a hood, a roof, or a decklid. This effect is very subjective. Because darker colors absorb more UV energy, lighter colors seem to weather better than darker ones.

Creating Sun Damage

1 *For the wear-damage panel, we sanded with our hands because we wanted a specific zone worn through. For the sun-damage panel, we want to sand a large area evenly, so we will start with 400-grit sandpaper wrapped around a soft sanding pad.*

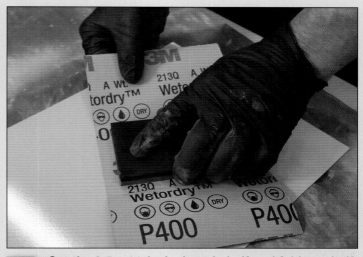

2 *This dual-density pad has a grey portion that is slightly softer than the black. Use the grey side against the panel to keep finger impressions from being ransferred through the sandpaper.*

3 *Cut the 8.5 x 11-inch sheet in half and fold one half into thirds. This will give you an easy way to hang on to the paper, and you will have multiple sides to switch to if your first side clogs or wears out.*

4 *Use a spray bottle with water and a few drops of soap mix (same as the wear-damage panel) to bricate the panel. Soak the panel and paper before arting to sand.*

5 *The yellow layer is thinner than the red or black and wears through quickly. It's important to monitor your progress and watch to see that you're sanding through very evenly for the sun-damage effect.*

Creating Sun Damage *continued*

6 A large area of the yellow is starting to become translucent, giving it a genuinely faded appearance. The degree of degradation is up to your personal taste. I've decided I want to expose more of the layers to simulate the sun damage example photo at the beginning of this chapter.

7 Wipe the residue away frequently to check your progress easily. Note the clamp holding the panel the table. The large contact area of the sanding pad and aggressive movement tended to push the panel across th table. Locking it down with the clamp made it easier to sand.

8 The black layer showing through the red is the sign to stop. I want to expose a lot of the red oxide. I want this layer to be removed evenly and carefully for a natural transition.

9 Use the same trifold method with the 600-grit pape on the same grey side of the sanding pad. The strategy here is to refine the scratches from the 400-grit step and make a gentler fade from layer to layer.

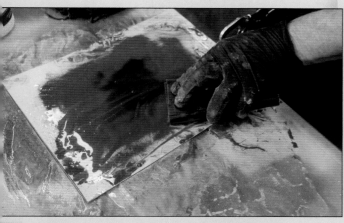

10 It doesn't take much sanding to reveal more of the black layer of primer. A few dozen strokes and there's a nice transition from red to black, as well as the red to yellow topcoat.

11 The effect I wanted is created, but I sanded too far and got right down to the bare metal. Part of the beauty of this process is that you can let mistakes work to your advantage. Over time, the bare steel would eventually rust and give another authentic representation of what might happen in nature, but we've got a trick to accelerate that process!

12 Vinegar is a mild acid that is safe to use. It will create oxidation very quickly, and bare metal will start to rust immediately. Spray a 50 percent vinegar and 50 percent water mix over the exposed bare metal.

13 To ensure the vinegar is forced into the pores of the metal, use a red scuffing pad and lightly sand the exposed metal only.

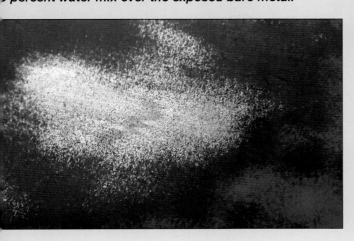

14 After about 30 seconds of exposure, the vinegar will take its toll. It will continue to rust at a fast rate. If you compare this effect to an actual vehicle panel, it's remarkably similar to the natural wear of original vintage paint.

Impact Damage

The leading edge of any vehicle panel takes a lot of abuse. Multiply that by time in service combined with the ravages of the sun, winters, road salts, and pilot errors, and you can see a recognizable patina and wear pattern. This is sometimes difficult to create and demands a bit of creativity to replicate a natural deterioration. When you inspect natural patina, take notes and make observations, and you'll soon have a reference guide with details such as the size of the rock chips and the condition of the paint around the chips. Seldom is there only one effect of time on an original panel.

What better way to simulate rock chip damage than with . . . well . . . a handful of rocks? These are crushed gravel picked up from the side of the road that is typically put down under pavement as a foundation. The great thing about this man-made crush is that the edges are random and typically sharp or pointed.

Creating Impact Damage

1 To create rock chip damage, drop stones onto the practice panel from about 12 to 15 inches above it. This is enough to chip the weak (spray can) paint in a very controlled manner. Drop the handful of rocks until you see a pattern similar to the impact damage on a rocker panel or the bottom of a fender edge.

2 The impact damage pattern is now in place, but the sheen on the panel is still there. This sheen makes the panel look simply damaged as opposed to damaged and aged. Another step is needed.

3 Using a sanding pad and 600-grit sandpaper, sand the entire surface evenly to knock the shine down. and through the raised edges of the chips. This will reate a more-pronounced chip with a shadow around it, aking it stand out better.

4 A paper towel removes the sanding sludge and allows you to check your progress. Check the effect often to see if it is authentic looking.

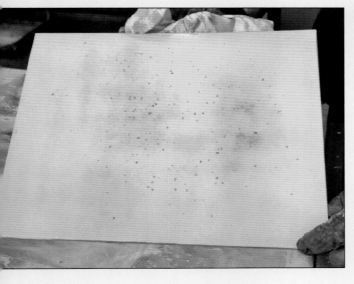

5 The goal was to have a mute gloss, a random faded look on the whole panel, and the look of a well-worn leading edge to a panel. This simple procedure took about 5 minutes in total and gave me exactly what I wanted to see.

Layers with Texture

Another way to create authentic atina is by creating texture in the round coats that are to be exposed. his lends character and dimension o the undercoats and gives more han just a faded layered appearance o your project.

Automotive spray painting was invented in the 1920s and implemented into automotive mass production in the 1930s. Through the 1940s and 1950s, the aftermarket repair techniques involved brushing on primer coatings, so there are many vehicles still around that were repaired and repainted using paintbrushes. This is probably not something that would fit into a 1960s muscle car, but an older 1930s or 1940s car might look period correct with a patina job using these techniques.

Understanding your methods in combination with planning out your goals is very important when considering what style of patina you want to create. Ultimately, it's up to you to fill in the blanks and create the history of your patina.

Creating Layers with Texture

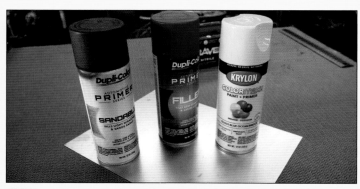

1 *Another version of layering involves creating texture to be exposed with sanding and surfacing. We'll use the same ground coats as our practice panels but a different topcoat color to demonstrate this technique. The black primer and the red oxide are from Dupli-Color. For the topcoat, we chose a pastel color that reminded us of the automotive stylings of the 1950s.*

2 *You will need a 20-gauge steel project panel, a chip brush, and a paint roller for this project.*

3 *Sand the panel with 220-grit paper. Typically, 220 grit is too aggressive for paint prep, but we want to create topography under the top layer of paint.*

4 *Apply the ground coat of black. I'm applying two very wet coats of black so I have a thick layer of paint that I can work with. You'll need a coating that is thick enough that you can texturize it in the next step.*

5 *With the paint still wet, quickly drag a pattern into the wet paint with a disposable chip brush. Don't remove any paint, just to make drag marks in the surface. The cheap brushes often leave hairs behind, which adds to the patina look.*

6 After the black ground coat has had 15 minutes of drying time, flood two very wet and full coats of red oxide primer onto the black surface. This primer dries very quickly, so the coats must be back-to-back with the can and nozzle very close to the surface so that the paint remains wet for the next step.

7 With the red oxide still very wet, use the paint roller to create a rough texture in the oxide primer. A few times across the surface is all it takes, and then let that coat dry.

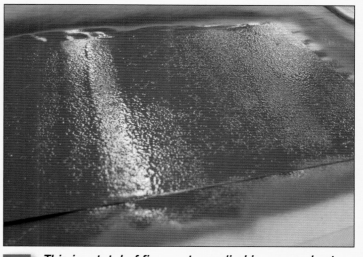

8 Flooding another wet coat in the rolled surface will fill in and flow out some of the texture but still give an interesting surface to reveal.

9 This is a total of five coats applied in a very short time. We definitely broke some rules here! We'll let this sit for at least 2 hours to properly allow solvents to evaporate from the coating.

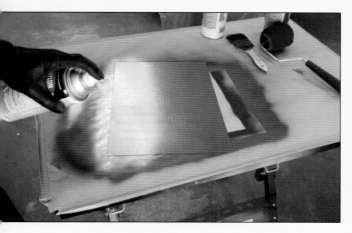

10 Once the red oxide is dry, apply two wet coats of the robin-egg color. Allow about 5 minutes drying time between coats.

Creating Layers with Texture *continued*

11 *The second coat is applied in the opposite direction as the first. Use a 50-percent overlap on each pass from about 5 inches above the panel.*

12 *Once the masterpiece has dried for at least an hou use a combination of 400-grit wet/dry sandpaper and slightly soapy water to begin exposing the layers. Start sanding in the middle of the panel.*

13 *Use the interface sanding pad to squeegee the water off and check your progress. You can now clearly see what the paint roller has created for texture in the red primer.*

14 *Sanding down through the red oxide to the black reveals the paint brush texture under the red. In th early days of vehicle production, many of the coatings were brushed on, and this technique is intended to imitat that time period.*

I've stumbled upon many of the techniques in this book by accident. Sometimes it's easy to get wrapped up in the stress of trying to make something perfect, but in most cases, especially in creating fauxtina, the imperfections look the most authentic. Nature is not perfectly symmetrical, sun damage depends on many things besides the sun, and the history and geography of a vehicle dictate the condition of antique objects. Try not to be careful when doir these exercises. You'll be pleasant surprised and empowered with wh you can create with some simp techniques.

PLANNING YOUR PAINT JOB

Every paint job has to start somewhere, just as every project has a starting point. The scope of the project may be dictated by the condition of the car, your budget, time availability, and skill level. A blank canvas is nice to have and leads to total freedom, but sometimes we need to draw influence from another subject. You can create a project goal based on a description or statement, but I find that it's much better to have a visual representation of what I want to create when it comes to paint jobs or vehicle design. This picture can come from anywhere: a car displayed at a car show, a pencil sketch, an image of a TV show vehicle, or photos from the internet.

Set Goals

I'm a visual learner and a visually inspired person. I get ideas from seeing things that I like and designs that someone else has done well. Sometimes a walk through a salvage yard or a used-car parking lot will serve me well as a way to get ideas for a project. Sometimes it's pure imagination. My point here is that you don't need divine inspiration to come up with something cool for your project nor do you have to borrow someone's ideas to start your own. Other people's excellence gets my creative juices going, and it inspires me to set goals for myself and to be as original as I can along the way.

Setting a visual goal is as important as a written statement, which is why so many custom car builders use a visual rendering as a guide through the course if the construction of a custom vehicle. Even if you decide to change the goal that you set along the way, you always have something to come back to. With a drawing or a photo of your project to go by, you have the ability to test colors and design for much less money than it would take to complete a paint job and be disappointed in it and have to redo it.

An artist's rendering is a nice luxury, and for me it's a justifiable expense when I'm building a car or

blank canvas is a great place to start! Although, creating a whole-image
atina look can seem overwhelming if you don't have a guide to start with or a
olid direction to move in. (Photo Courtesy Steve Longacre)

This digital drawing is by Steve Longacre of Preferredline Media. Steve is a talented artist, and he used some ideas I shared with him to come up with an excellent representation of what I want to guide me through my paint job. The drawing shows rust spots, wear items, wheel choices, and even custom details from the actual vehicle, such as the signal light delete on the front fenders.

Another huge advantage of getting a digital rendering is the ability to change colors and test different color combinations without spending any time on the vehicle or any money on paint. Starting over costs a lot of time, and money spent on materials and can be a serious drain on your inspiration! Whatever your guide is, make sure you have the opportunity to visualize the outcome before you begin the process. (Photo Courtesy Steve Longacre)

Line art is available online in thousands of different drawings. Search online art by typing "line art" and your vehicle's make in a popular search engine. I typed in "VW Bug line art" and seconds later the computer gave me pages and pages of drawings from every angle I could imagine. Print out an image and use markers to create a great visualization of your project. (Photo Courtesy Steve Longacre)

There may be online services that ca[n] get you what you need for inspiration Spend some time looking to see wha[t] is available online; you may be surprised what kind of deals you can ge[t] on personalized art!

refinishing one for a client. You can ask an artist to draw specific features and colors and customize them in a very detailed manner, but that luxury comes at a price. A digital artist might charge $300 to $500 per view, so if you want a front three-quarter view as well as a rear view, you've just spent $1,000. If your budget is not that flush, Photoshop can be a great way to make changes on your own and with very little expense. With the power of good editing software, an artist is able to easily change colors to give us options and alternate views.

Websites such as fiverr.com an[d] Etsy.com are loaded with artists an[d] hobbyists who advertise many di[f]ferent services. I've personally foun[d] many resources for creating dig[i]tal art, voiceover files, video edit[-]ing, and even digital designs tha[t] are very affordable through the[se] nline service websites. Do some nternet searches on sites that adver- se digital services, and you may be oth inspired and surprised at the eals you can get on project vehicle nderings.

Find Inspiration

Part of your homework, other than learning paint chemistry and application techniques, is to seek out sources that will give you inspi-

ration for your patina project. That doesn't necessarily mean old cars. Everyday objects that are dated or worn can serve as models and authentic representations of how natural aging looks. I've got an old

n always on the lookout for cool old cars because there are always interesting things to see, no matter what the condi- on. Every vehicle patinas differently, and it's fun to get perspective on all the details of the aging process, especially on ojects like this one.

is emblem is still firmly attached to the fender of this 950s Chevrolet, but the chrome has bubbled and is bent. is is a perfect example of what a truly worn-out badge n look like naturally and great inspiration for how you n add realism to your project.

This vintage pocket knife has seen better days, but it hints at a long history. The over-sharpened rusty blades and the grit that has been jammed down into the bone handle are classic patina and beautiful to me. Old cars are no differ- ent. There's always opportunity to imagine a past life and add interest to your project.

This VW half cab is a parts car now, but there are interesting rust spots and trim pieces that we can borrow styling from.

This F150 still has its original paint and is very solid. It needs a tune-up and new side glass and it could be on the road as a true survivor. For me, it was an opportunity to see how black fades and how the rust turns the black a dark blue color as the oxides mask the pigment.

Heavy equipment ages before its time, at least when it comes to the finish! This bulldozer was covered in beautiful patina that showed me aged lettering and other authentic wear.

The transition from rust to paint is dramatic and sudden. No airbrush fading here.

The back side of this blade is a beautiful combination of rust, flaked and scratched paint, and a thin layer of dirt that creates a lot of texture. Notice the crusty grease stacked up by the hydraulic rams behind the blade itself. These are all important details to have documented if you want realism in your patina.

ocket knife with a fake antler han-e that is beautifully exposing the astic under the paint in the grain the antler material. The matte fin-h gives way to a shiny area where e paint is rubbed off and dirt and ebris (yuck) is driven down into the lleys and recesses, creating a vari-y of finishes, textures, and glosses.

One day, I came across an older illdozer sitting in a field. I was ken by the worn paint on the steel ody. While the color is not neces-rily something I gravitate to, it as authentic natural patina, so I ok some pictures of it for future spiration.

Create a Photo Reference Library

Notice details on items all around u. Take notes, and more impor-ntly, create a library of authentic tina photos that you can draw ference from when it comes to the ler points of detailing your proj-t. Digital technology is a wonder-l resource that you can use to your vantage to create a library of exam-es to create your own unique style patina. If you don't have a digital mera, use your mobile phone to eate your photo library. It's easy to irt a category or named file to col-t photos for future reference.

Going to a local car show or rs-n-coffee event will no doubt ow you to photograph patina hicles or original paint exam-es. Just driving down some rural ads will most likely yield results of ture or neglect in a paint job that u can photograph. Either way you cide to collect photographs to ide you, it's simple to assemble a llection of photos that can serve your personal roadmap and guide

My phone goes everywhere with me. It has a large storage capacity for pho-tos and videos, but it's also connected to the web and cloud-based services where I can store pictures and access them from any number of devices. Dig-ital images are basically free, and the cameras in smartphones can produce professional-quality pictures and video these days.

Collecting your own photos into a personal database can bypass any copyright issues you may run into by collecting images off the internet. There are strict rules about using public images for professional gain or even sharing online, so make sure you get per-mission to use other peo-ple's intellectual property.

to creating your brand and style of patina.

The library can also be an incred-ible resource for archived and accu-rate photos of period-correct painted antiques. If you are not planning on monetizing images that may be copyrighted, there are no issues with photographing cataloged images from a library to compile your inspiration file. Just be aware that published photos are copyright property of the photographer and that you may need to request writ-ten permission if you plan on using the images in any commercial or public way. A different approach and one more personal is to create your

own database of images, notes, and tutorials. These can be contained on a separate file in your computer, a cell phone, or a cloud service, all of which can be easily accessible with today's technology.

Photo Project

As part of the planning process, it is helpful to assemble a portfolio of effects that you want to recreate with every angle represented: front, top, sides, rear, as well as details of the type of patina that you want to see on your project. You can cre-ate a collage of images to use as a vision board of sorts or for quick reference.

Typically, I think through all aspects of a vehicle project during the planning stage, not just the finish or paint job. It is all relevant to the overall goal. Wheel choices, interior colors, accessories, and even performance goals all have to fit an overall project theme. Treat this like a fun thing! It's a lot of work, but the more time you put in on the front end, the more organized you'll be during the process and you can spend a little more time on the fun parts of doing this!

Develop a Painting Strategy

The art of patina paint comes down to a very simple concept: artificially expose underlying layers of paint to simulate age, deterioration, and wear. To effectively have control over this method, you must understand the system of layers of paint finish in order to reveal them and their contrasting colors in a precise and controlled manner.

Is your car a survivor? Or has it been repaired? There are two distinctly different strategies involved with each of these goals. A survivor will have continuity on every panel, faded spots that match up from corner to corner, and will look as if the vehicle has been intact from its beginning. A patched-up Frankenstein collection of used parts can have its own unique appeal, giving the illusion of a work in progress or a vehicle that's limping and waiting to die.

If you're still old school and want tangible files and photos, then a three-ring binder can be a great project planner and reference tool. I've got my favorite patina pics for all the aspects of my project, and I can keep it on hand as I paint my car.

The fender on this truck tells me that it has had a lot of work done under the hood. There is a mostly red oxide undercoat here that gives way to surface rust of the sheet metal, and it's randomly worn in different places. The ground coat here would be black followed by red oxide and then a thin coat of blue topcoat on the perimeter of the panels.

Patina can and does have many forms. Some vehicles look correct with a replaced panel, as in the case of this barn-find 196 Mustang Fastback. We wanted this car to look as if somebody replaced a damaged fender with one from a salvage yard so they could continue driving. The fender in primer, combined with other patina paint techniques, gave an authentic look. (Photo Courtesy Melissa Cross)

Choose a Period

A big decision, and a very personal decision at that, is deciding what style of patina you want to copy.

Choosing a period-correct style for your vehicle is as important as your color choice if your goal is authentic aging. Mid-1950s cars are usually solid colors, and there were a lot of pastel and primary colors on many vehicles, which contributes to the identity of that era. One wouldn't find clearcoat delamination on a 1955 Chevrolet. Along the same line, a mid-1990s F150 wouldn't have a red oxide undercoat and fade from robin-egg blue to the red oxide on the top surfaces.

Internet image searches are a good resource, but actually seeing genuine patina is the best way to get a sense on the natural deterioration of paint and the subtle way that time exposes the layers of underlying paint and primers. Most original paint jobs have a contrasting color or an undercoat, but not always. Undercoats vary between models, years, and makes. Just because a certain make came from the factory with a black primer doesn't necessarily mean that you have to repeat the recipe. You can color coordinate your layers to make things more natural or just because it is your personal preference.

Make a Plan

Having finished several full patina paint jobs, I've learned a few tricks. One of the most valuable revelations I've had is that one needs to consider the amount of work it's going to take to expose the underlying layers of color and contrast and plan for that carefully when designing the paint job. For example, if I want the top of a vehi-

This VW bug has a 20-year-old paint job that is wearing badly and is delaminating. The clearcoat separates from the color due to UV damage and oxidation between the layers. This is not something you'd want to see on an early 1960s bug, so choose your effects and your patina decades wisely!

Undercoats

Red oxide undercoats seem to blend extremely well with light colored topcoats, such as whites, greens, blues. Black undercoats work well with reds, yellows, and most other colors, and the combinations are somewhat pleasing. It's up to you to create the illusion of faded paint the way you want to see it. ■

There are four distinct tones of color here on the roof of this 1964 Chevrolet truck. The faded red at the edges and the sealer coat under the red fades out to the grey primer overtop of the original black sealer the truck received at the factory.

If I'm recreating this look, I really have to paint the outside edges of the panel only with the final topcoat color.

cle to show *most* of the undercoat through a faded topcoat the strategy is to apply a *very* thin layer of paint over the undercoat in areas that I want to sand through and expose it and apply paint heavier on the edges, where I know that the sun wouldn't have oxidized quite as much due to the angles. This technique allows me to quickly achieve

the effect easily and, most importantly, evenly.

When you design your paint strategy, you must consider if the ground coats are compatible with your chosen topcoat color. It doesn't have to be "correct" according to naturally worn colors or cars, it just has to make sense to you and give you the tools to create the effect you want.

Don't think so much in the beginning of your plan about the glass or rust streaks off of the window corners. Those details are tools to enhance the patina effect. There are many cool details and layers that you can use on top of your base paint job with airbrush, templates, sign paint-ing techniques, and even decals if you choose, but your strategy has to start with what's underneath every-thing. Your plan must provide the basis and foundation to an overall color scheme.

Your plan can be yours. You don't have to follow anyone else's conven-tion. Use this book to learn creativ[e] techniques so you can whip up yo[ur] own blend of patina that becomes yo[ur] design and art. With a little researc[h,] creating practice panels, and creativit[y,] you can come up with a way to pati[na] your vehicle to represent whatev[er] nostalgia you want to subscribe to.

The wear on this top is uneven. The car probably sat partially covered for years so that the driver's side faded faster than the passenger's side. Another possibility is that the paint job in 1963 was applied by people on an assem-bly line (not by today's robotic technology), and the paint may be thicker and stronger on the passenger's side.

This is original patina on this Dodge 300. The red oxide i[s] striking and very even in color and tone. This effect woul[d] be very simple to recreate due to the simplicity of the col[or] scheme and the division between the green, grey, and re[d.]

The black undercoat on this mid-1980s Chevrolet truck is obvious in this picture. There is an interesting mix of exposed undercoat, probably from decades of gasoline exposure, as well as the rust on the flared-out bed side in front of the wheel arch. The starting point to all of these effects would definitely be a black ground coat of primer.

This is a beautifully styled 1969 Chevrolet truck. The mod-ern wheels look great against the aged paint, but the tea[l] color is vivid, telling me that it has been artfully reapplie[d] in the style of the rest of the patina.

CREATING COLORS

Colors have an influence over how we feel. It's a common understanding that color affects everything from our moods to our perception of quality. Color is very important in all forms of advertisement and sales, and a simple color change on a product can make the difference of a popular item or one that sits on a shelf. There is an inherent understanding about the relationship between color and the perception of quality in any item. It's no accident that color creates fashion trends and leads the way in marketing strategies regardless of platform.

It is critical to understand how paint fades and color changes in order to create the illusion of patina with new paint. Armed with this knowledge, we can figure out how to create the colors we want that look authentically faded right from the start.

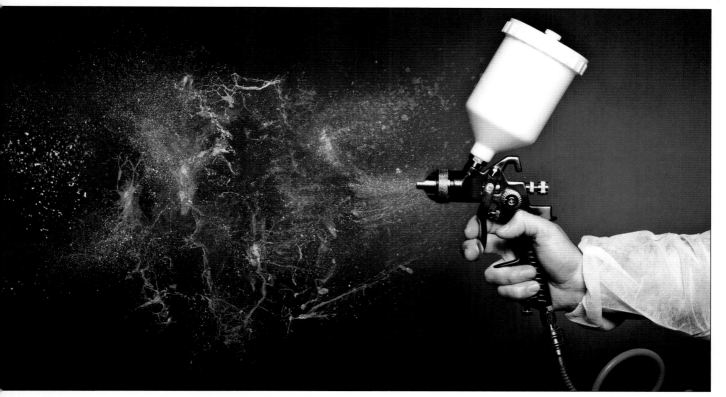

Color tells a story all by itself. Pastel colors bring us back to the 1950s, and different tones can remind us of personal experiences from the past. Color has power!

Understanding Color

In the case of patina, muted colors make us nostalgic and reminiscent of the past. There is typically a softness to color that creates a worn-out look, especially with automotive paints. In the case of metals, such as copper, brass, or aluminum, patina takes on a powdery look and changes the color of the metal itself (at least the top layer that is affected by the atmosphere and chemicals in the air). It's important for us to understand why colors fade if we are going to create the appearance of faded colors.

Fading

Oxidation occurs on the top layers of paint, much like rust occurs on the top layer of steel. As paint fades (oxidizes), hydrogen and oxygen molecules attack the pigment and resins in the paint film. If left unattended, oxidation on paint will dive deeper and deeper and finally reveal undercoats or even the bare metal beneath the coatings themselves.

During the fading process, the pigments tend to lighten up and go to a more opaque and milkier appearance. This is caused by the oxidized filter of degraded paint that sits between the paint and the atmosphere. The more paint fades, the weaker it gets, and the faster it will fade out again after polishing.

Color Influence

Colors also influence each other. A bright red panel placed right beside a white panel will give the impression of a slightly darker and redder tone to the white panel. A yellow panel placed beside a white panel gives the illusion that the white is slightly more yellow than it actually is. This is due to how colors observed together are averaged out as they're processed through our eyes to our brain.

Another example of color influence is using a ground coat color that is darker or lighter than the topcoat. This is common practice in the custom painting world, where a white ground coat is used to make colors appear more vivid. This effect is caused by the opacity or translucent nature of some colors, particularly reds. Ferrari red (Rosa Red) over a white ground coat appears brighter than it will over a black ground coat. Over black, reds take on a slightly browner look due to yellow tints that are present in black colors. Using a white ground coat under a robin's-egg blue or turquoise will make the green tones appear brighter. You can influence the feel of your paint job by using certain colors for ground coats, primers, and topcoats. Take your time when making decisions about your color.

The Color Wheel

You may want to simply enhance the color that your car or truck came with from the factory. If that's the case, you will need to pay close attention to how age affects that particular color so you can tap into the nuance and be authentic in creating your patina. If you're starting from scratch with an all-over paint job, you'll have the luxury (and responsibility) of designing the complete color palate. There are tools that will help in understanding how color looks faded, what direction it takes (lighter darker, greener, bluer), and how to interpret how color ages naturally.

All color is derived of the three primary colors: red, blue, and yellow. If you've ever looked at a color and thought that the yellow you're looking at seemed greener than a different yellow or that a blue looked more purple than another blue, you've witnessed color direction. Aristotle and Sir Isaac Newton set the standard that there are seven recognized colors in the spectrum of light: red, orange, yellow, green, blue, indigo, and violet, in that order. This is the direction of the colors recognized in a rainbow.

As mentioned in chapter 2, the acronym ROYGBIV (pronounced Roy-Gee-Biv) is an easy way to memorize the colors of the spectrum. If you've viewed sunlight through an acrylic prism or if you've ever seen a rainbow on a horizon (or even in a garden sprinkler), you've seen a natural color spectrum. These colors are also represented in photography or videography when referring to color temperature.

A color wheel shows you a literal interpretation of how each primary color fits into the color spectrum and how one influences the color on either side of it. The exact blend of one primary color with another is called a secondary color. Looking

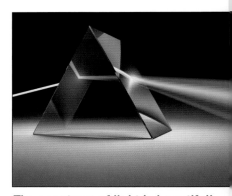

The spectrum of light is beautiful! When light is refracted through a crystal prism, every color of the rainbow is created. The spectrum is also a tool that can be used to understand color and the relationship of one color to the next.

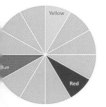  

...u can see the three primary colors ... the left side of this diagram: red, ...ue, and yellow. When these colors ...e blended together, secondary ...lors are created, as seen on the ...ght. These drawings represent the ...sic rules of color mixing, and what ... accepted color science today. For ...ample, blue mixed with yellow ...akes green.

The color wheel is believed to have been created and put into use as a tool in the mid-1600s based on Isaac Newton's studies on white light. A one-dimensional color wheel is the spectrum of color in a circle to demonstrate how one color compares to another and how colors are combined to create shades and variations. Today, it's a wonderful reference guide for creating our own blends of color.

...color wheel, you can begin to see ...here these colors come from and ...ow they're the product of blending ...imary colors.

When I'm working with colors, ...hether tinting or creating, I have a ...lor wheel close by as a reminder of ...ow colors react with each other. In ...y shop, there is a large poster of a ...lor wheel beside my paint mixing ...stem that is an excellent guide to ref-...ence color intensity and direction.

Color Tinting

Now that you have some background on the three primary colors and how the color wheel works, you can start to work with color tinting. Experimenting with the three primary colors (red, blue, and yellow), will show you how to change the colors and see their direction. You can teach yourself how to make a red "bluer" or a yellow "greener," which

will show you how to properly tint color to correct it for your patina job later and to create secondary colors of the tints of your paint job.

Acrylic colors are vivid and very inexpensive to buy at a hobby store. There will be many different color variations and shades to choose from; for these exercises, choose the three basic colors to blend together. You will also need an inexpensive scale that will give you a unit measurement; in our case, we're using grams as our unit of measurement. We recommend measuring the colors as they're blended in order to have control over the outcome. This will give you a lot of information and will help in correcting a color that you're trying to recreate.

Creating Secondary Colors

We were trying to create the secondary colors violet, green and orange. We mixed equal parts of each color, but they didn't quite turn out as we expected. By looking at the color wheel, we can see what direction we need to take to

Mixing Violet

Our goal here will be to try to create the secondary colors of violet, green, and orange. You will need the paint, a scale, and mixing cups.

1 *Our inexpensive scale is quite accurate to the 100th of a gram. The stainless cups are inexpensive easy to clean, and compatible with any type of paint. The paints are acrylic concentrates made for crafts and painting.*

Mixing Violet *continued*

2 To get an accurate measurement of our paint and not the mixing cup, place the cup on the scale and wait for it to settle.

3 With the cup on the scale, zero out the measurement by hitting the T button, which stands for "tare. This ensures that only the weight of the paint we put in the cup will be measured, not the weight of the cup.

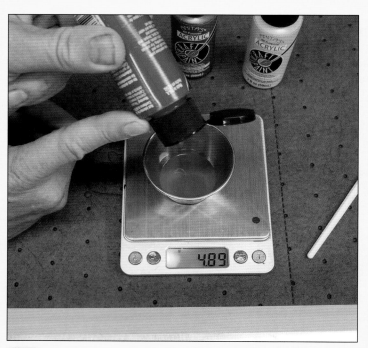

4 Next, add 5 grams of red paint to the cup. Each drop weighs about 0.5 gram, so slow down when the scale is close to the final weight.

5 Once the scale says 5 grams, tare it again so we're only measuring paint and not the cup. This keeps the measuring very simple.

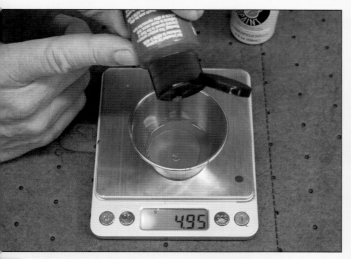

6 Next, add 5 grams (equal parts) of blue to the red. As you can see, our blue is not a true blue, but a ghter shade. This needs to be considered when blending lors. This was the closest tint to true blue in this particu-r color palate. In fact, it was actually named "true-blue," en though it doesn't have the intensity of a true primary lor. It will serve our purposes in this experiment.

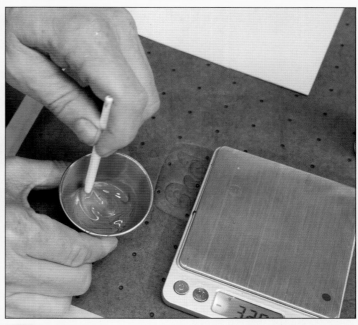

7 With the colors combined, blend them together. You can see the definite violet tone, but it is a subtle color and not a true purple, much like the blue.

Mixing Green

1 Place the next cup in the center of the scale, and zero the scale by hitting the tare button.

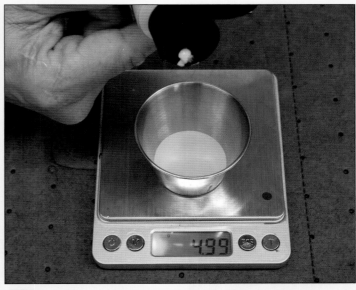

2 Add 5 grams of yellow. The acrylic paint is very thick, and it's sometimes difficult to get a precise measurement dispensed into the cup. Since this is a color test, if we're very close to the actual gram weight, we will still have an accurate ratio with each color for comparison.

Mixing Green *continued*

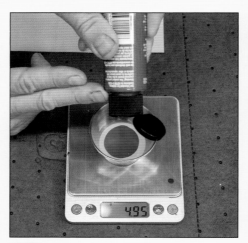

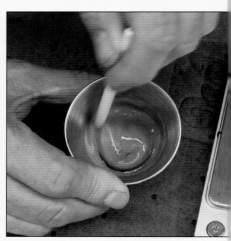

3 *Again, tare the scale so you only measure the added paint.*

4 *Add 5 grams of blue. We're using equal parts of yellow and blue to make green. In theory, equal parts should get us right in the middle of each primary color, which should be a nice green.*

5 *After blending the two colors, we have a bluish green that surprised us a little. We were expecting an apple green, but we suspect that the odd light blue color is the cause of the weird green tone.*

Mixing Orange

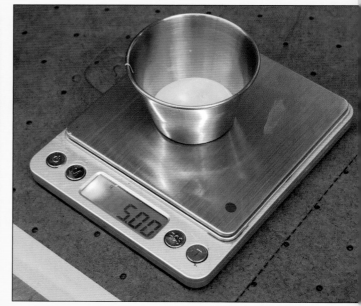

1 *With a new cup, tare the scale and add 5 grams of yellow paint. We will blend yellow and red to make orange, another secondary color.*

2 *Tare the scale again.*

Add 5 grams of red to the cup. The red and yellow colors look like they're true primary colors.

4 Blend the red and yellow together thoroughly, making sure there is no pigment in the bottom of the cup or on the sides, as this could influence the color.

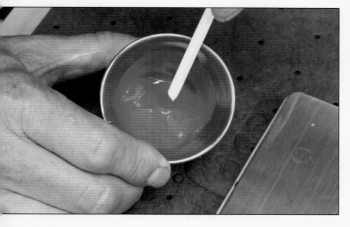

5 Rather than orange, we seem to have a pastel red, which tells us that our 50:50 ratio, at least with these particular colors, will not give us the secondary colors we were hoping for.

eate the colors we are looking for. mixing more of one color and less another, will adjust our colors to at we want to see. For example, en we mixed yellow and red to get ange, it made a lighter pastel red. en you look at the color wheel to d a true orange color, you will see that it's not directly in the middle of the yellow and red. It is much more on the yellow side. This tells us how to create the color we want by simply using a different ratio of one color to the next. To get a better and more accurate orange, add less of the red to the yellow.

Tinting Your Colors

To continue practicing color tinting, look at the color wheel for each of the three secondary color examples we just created. For each, you can see that you need less of one of the primary colors to get a more accurate version of a secondary color. Let's try it.

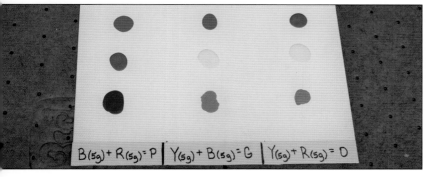

$B_{(5g)} + R_{(5g)} = P$ | $Y_{(5g)} + B_{(5g)} = G$ | $Y_{(5g)} + R_{(5g)} = O$

We placed samples on a neutral background to show what we created. A 50:50 ratio gives us a pastel version of violet, green, and orange. Good information! However, they are not the colors we wanted to create.

Remixing Violet

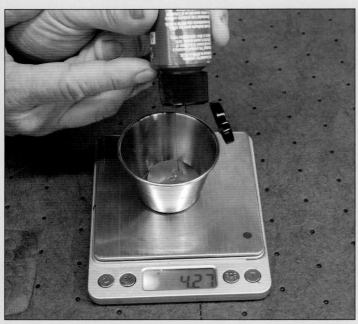

1 Let's try to get a better purple! After taring the scale, add 5 grams of blue in the cup.

2 Zero the scale before adding the red. For this blend we're changing the ratio a little after looking at the color wheel.

3 The color wheel shows a little more blue in the mix will result in a more vivid purple or violet. There's a narrow band of the dark purple next to the blue, and that tells us that we need more of the blue color in the ratio. For this tint, use 25 percent of the red. To arrive at the correct amount of red, use a calculator and multiply 5.0 by 25 percent (0.25). Our calculator tells us that this is 1.25 grams.

4 After blending the two colors, we get a much more accurate violet color! This is still not a vivid purple, but it resembles the muted tone and dirtiness of the blue were using, so this is not surprising.

Remixing Green

1 To make a better green, start off with 5 grams of yellow paint only in the mixing cup.

2 Taring the scale is important! It's easy to skip this step and just start pouring, which will ruin the experiment and totally change your results.

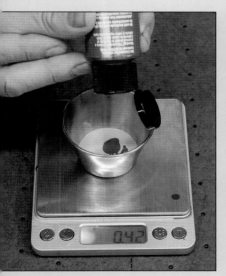

3 This time, try using 10 percent of the blue. Use the calculator and multiply 5.0 by 10 percent (0.10). Add 0.5 grams of blue with the hopes of getting a more accurate green color.

4 We're mixing thoroughly again! Make sure that all of the color is blended and picked up from the bottom and sides. A color mix is only as accurate as the one mixing it.

5 Although not an apple green, this blend is definitely more of a true green than the last attempt.

Remixing Orange

1 After zeroing the scale, start with a fresh 5 grams of yellow to try for a more conventional orange tone.

2 Reset the scale to zero to mix accurately!

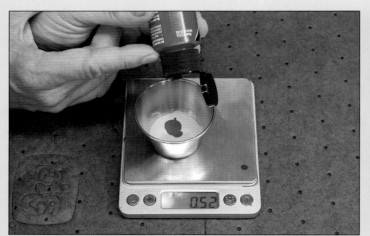

3 You can see that true orange is closer to the yellow color than right in the middle of yellow and red on the color wheel, so we've substantially reduced the amount of red in this blend. Let's use only 10 percent of the red color to try and make orange. To arrive at the correct amount of red, use a calculator and multiply 5.0 by 10 percent (0.10). Add 0.5 gram of red.

4 This time we're seeing a much better representatio of orange after it is mixed! Now we know the direction we need to go in on the color wheel to change to tone of the orange from pastel to bright orange.

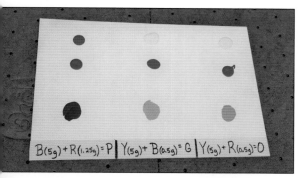

$$B(5g) + R(1.25g) = P \quad | \quad Y(5g) + B(0.5g) = G \quad | \quad Y(5g) + R(0.5g) = O$$

Here are the results of our blends from top to bottom. You can read the ratio at the bottom and see what it took to get the different tones of color. Here's an interesting footnote, we let the colors sit for an hour before looking at them, and they were slightly different colors when they were dry. Some of the brightness was gone, but the color was richer and closer to what we wanted. It's a good policy when blending color to wait until it has dried fully to judge it.

The end result of all of these tint exercises is that you have used the three primary colors to create secondary colors and demonstrated ROYGBIV. A patina paint job is totally unique, so why not invest the time into making your own unique color? This can be a great conversation piece, as well as something you can be very proud of when your paint job is finished. Ultimately, this will be your art, so personalize it with your own color!

1974 VW Beetle Patina Project

To show a full patina paint job from start to finish, we chose the 1974 Volkswagen Beetle. It may look familiar from the artist renderings earlier in this chapter. These cars have great character with some of the same characteristics as 1940s to 1950s–era cars with rounded fenders and roofline.

Our artist's rendering shows a faded white side insert mixed with a turquoise main color that is covered in patina and surface rust. There are a number of ways to get close to those colors: use color guides, use factory-mixed colors, or pay someone to custom blend a color for you. All of these options can get expensive, depending on the type of paint you use, and you still may have to settle for a color that's close to what you want instead of exactly what you're looking for. Keep that in mind as you are planning your project.

The Dupli-Color Paint Shop system that we are using for this project is very affordable and simple to use. It requires no hardener or catalyst, comes mixed in the can and ready to spray, and is much safer to use than a lot of professional paints. This system has its limitations as well, since it is factory packaged with fewer than 20 pre-mixed colors. Unless you get creative, you don't have many options other than what is provided by the manufacturer.

Interestingly enough, the Dupli-Color system had all of the basic primary colors we needed to blend our own turquoise color using the techniques we used. The steps that follow walk you through the entire paint color creation process for our VW project. ∎

There are thousands of pre-mixed colors of every hue available from body shop supply stores or online vendors. Color-chip books show a color code for foreign and domestic cars, and a little research can get you a mixing formula for classic or modern colors for any vehicle from the 1920s on. This is a safe way to guarantee the color you want to see on your project, but understanding basic color theory can give you the tools needed to make your own color if you choose.

1974 VW Beetle Patina Project Continued

1 Our color design for the Bug was simple and required only a few colors. The Dupli-Color Paint Shop system has all the primary colors plus white, which gives us everything we need to create our own signature color. Dupli-Color also has a nice matte clearcoat that is perfect for sealing in the patina styling.

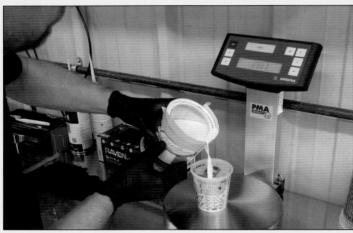

2 We used Championship White as a base, since our turquoise is very light. We used round numbers that were easy to multiply to make a simple formula for our color. We poured 100 grams into a half-pint mixing cup.

3 The colors needed to be stirred thoroughly before they were poured in. This is very important as a rule with paint but absolutely critical when formulating colors because the pigments settle quickly.

4 The homemade pour spout is just a simple piece of 1.5-inch masking tape with a V cut out of it. This directs the fluid in a straight line. It works very well when pouring from full cans.

5 We tared the scale for accuracy before adding anything in.

6 We started with 20 grams each of yellow and blue, starting with Deep Blue, to see what we ended up with. These larger scales are more convenient with a larger volume being mixed, but the small ones are less expensive and work just as well.

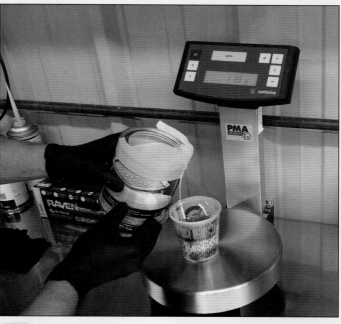

7 We added 20 grams of Chrome Yellow to the blue. We were aiming for a light green that we could then tint to our preference.

8 We wanted to be exact on our measurement, so we stopped just short of 20 grams and used a pipette to drizzle in the rest. Pipettes can be purchased hobby stores or paint supply stores.

9 Surprisingly, our color is fairly close right away, but we wanted a slightly richer color. Our color wheel told us that we needed a little more blue to get a rich turquoise.

1974 VW Beetle Patina Project *Continued*

10 *We used a pipette to add in another 17 grams of Deep Blue.*

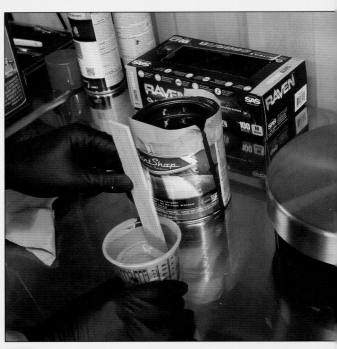

11 *The mix in the cup looked close. Wet paint looks different in the cup than it will dry on a panel, so we decided it was time to do a spray-out panel as a serious test.*

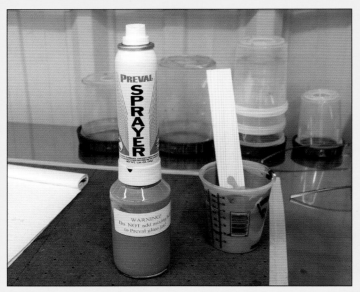

12 *The Preval Sprayer is a reusable air-charged canister that allows a paint jar to screw on to the bottom. This allows you to spray paint without being connected to an airline setup, making color testing easy.*

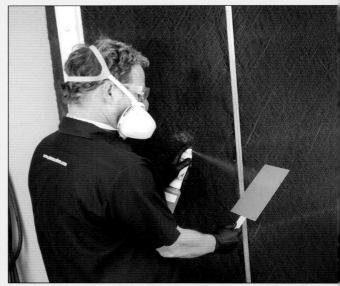

13 *Using a 50-percent overlap on a spray-out card, we sprayed three coats of our mix on the card, allowing 5 minutes to dry between coats. Already the color looks richer!*

14 *Even before it was dry, our color test looked deeper than it did in the bucket. As paint dries, it lightens up and evens out. It took three wet coats to get complete coverage. This is not uncommon; most automotive paint colors have opacity and are designed to take several coats to achieve full coverage.*

15 *For our second color of the two-tone paint job, we wanted an antique white. We started with 100 grams of Championship White.*

16 *My years of mixing automotive paint tell me that antique and ivory whites have a small amount of yellow in the formula, so we added two tenths of a gram (.2g) to 100 grams of Championship White to see what we have.*

17 *It didn't take much to get close in the cup, but you can't tell until you spray it out on a panel in multiple coats and take a look.*

1974 VW Beetle Patina Project *Continued*

18 We masked off half of the turquoise spray-out panel and painted the lower half with three coats of our tinted white. We waited 5 minutes between each coat.

19 When we compare our spray out to the digital rendering, its exactly what we wanted! Placing the sample against the actual car we're going to paint, style affirms things again. We have our final paint formula! These colors didn't exist yesterday, and now we've got a simple formula to make them any time we choose.

PAINT FORMULA VW PROJECT (Using Dupli-Color Paint Shop System)	
Tarnished Turquoise	**(Quart)**
Championship White	500 grams
Chrome Yellow	100 grams
Deep Blue	185 grams
Matte Clear	115 grams
Washout White	**(Quart)**
Championship White	800 grams
Chrome Yellow	1.6 grams
Matte Clear	98.4 grams

20 Our notes show that we have very simple numbers to use to scale the formula up. We named our color "Tarnished Turquoise." To get the color, we mixed a blend of 157 grams, so it's a matter of some simple multiplication to mix larger volumes. To get nearly a full quart, all we have to do is multiply our formula by 5 and we'll have 785 grams, which is just short of a quart. We'll use the Paint Shop Matte Clear to add in another 115 grams to make up the difference and create a complete quart formula. For our color called "Washout White," we'll use 800 grams of Championship White and add just 1.6 grams of Chrome Yellow, making up the difference with another 98.4 grams of clear to equal a full quart. This will give us a very accurate color mix for both colors that is simple to mix, and easily repeatable, since we may need as much as a gallon of color to do our all-over paint job on the bug.

CREATING PATINA ON METAL, PLASTIC, AND GLASS

Now that we have covered creating our paint colors, let's talk about creating patina effects. Metal is the primary substrate in which we may want to instigate rust to create a patina effect. Rusty metal is the foundation for many automotive fauxtina projects, and the aesthetic foundation of the entire "Rat-Rod" style of custom car building in the automotive aftermarket. The act of taking a decades-worn vehicle and enhancing the deteriorated metal and paint has become a genre of custom car creation, and it bears acknowledgment and legitimate praise in the industry for expanding the way cars and customizing can be appreciated.

These processes take a lot of time in nature. Thick iron beams will remain strong for hundreds of years while steadily rusting. Copper or bronze will slowly change outer coloration and develop beautiful patina over the years. We simply don't have another 50 or 60 years to let vehicles ferment and degrade, so we must come up with techniques to accelerate time or fool the eye to give the appearance that we have. A simpler, more natural, and more passive approach to accelerated rusting simply involves exposing the metal to chemicals and letting time and chemistry take its toll, although not the decades-long time frames that nature demands.

Basic Chemistry

Oxidation is not always rust colored on iron. In most cases, the oxidation process will deteriorate completely through the metal, the top layer will flake off and expose underlying iron, and it will eventually disintegrate completely. Copper oxidation (such as the green patina on the Statue of Liberty) bonds to the base metal and forms a protective layer on top, creating a chemical seal against the outside atmosphere and slowing or stopping the deterioration process. You can speed up the process of rusting with acids and salts to create the appearance of natural exposure.

Adding an acid to metal produces hydrogen gas, which promotes faster oxidation. When you add a couple of tablespoons of salt to a cup of a mild acid, such as vinegar, you create a very corrosive solution that can then be sprayed onto bare metal products, such as fasteners and hinges. If you then have a container of ammonia sitting beside the coated parts, the fumes will affect the sprayed solution and set in motion a chemical reaction that will deteriorate the outside surfaces of these metals very quickly.

Ventilation

Please take all precautions to maintain a well-ventilated area and to use appropriate safety equipment while mixing chemicals. While we show you how to mix certain simple chemicals together to gain an effect on metal, certain reactions could occur if care is not taken to be safe. Take the warning labels on these household items seriously! Have fun with this, but please stay safe. ■

This will create the appearance that a particular part has been rusting for a very long time.

Accelerated Rusting

By using basic chemistry and common products, we can create a cool rusted surface that looks as if it has been rusting for years. Vinegar is a mild acid, ammonia is a common household cleaner, and table salt has obviously been around for millennia as a spice and flavor enhancement. Individually, they are benign components, but once we put chemistry to work, they work with and against each other to give us great rusty results!

To demonstrate how to create patina, we will apply some simple household chemicals to a small piece of 20-gauge bare steel. Please b[e] aware that even though these prod[-]ucts are available over the counte[r] mixing acids and corrosive elemen[ts] can potentially cause harm or seriou[s] injury. Appropriate safety equipmen[t] is always necessary. Wear glove[s] safety glasses, and protective cloth[-]ing in a well-ventilated area whe[n] practicing this method.

Accelerating the Rusting Process

1 Our chemistry experiment involves very simple components: vinegar, ammonia, and simple table salt. You also need plastic mixin[g] pails and a plastic spoon to ensure that no unexpected results occur. Our 20-gauge steel sample is cleaned but untreated and unsanded.

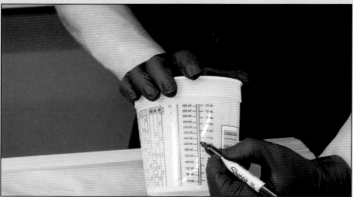

2 Add 12 ounces of distilled vinegar to the mixing cup. Vinegar is a mild acid, and in its distilled form, it is reduced to 5-percent acidity. This will normally produce a nice patina if given enough time in a very safe manner, but we're pushing the envelope in this case.

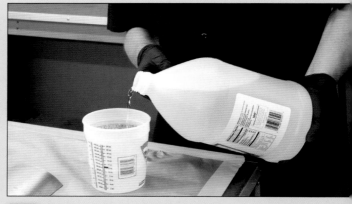

3 Wear gloves and safety glasses while pouring, just as a good practice. Bodyshop etiquette serves man[y] purposes, one of which is obviously safety. Controlling your environment is another so you can safely track result[s] and repeat them later.

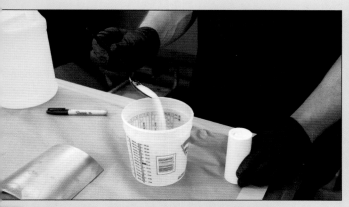

4 Next, add 2 tablespoons of regular iodized table salt to the vinegar. This creates a much more aggressive solution. On a very small scale, adding the salt (sodium chloride) creates a mild hydrochloric acid that acts much more aggressively when it comes in contact with a metal surface.

5 Blend the salt and vinegar together thoroughly until you don't see any salt in the bottom of the mixing bucket.

6 Using a brush, cloth, or sponge, completely wet the surface of the metal. This begins the chemical process of accelerated oxidation. You'll probably notice an immediate effect of the metal "brightening" as it gets wet with the vinegar solution. This particular mix is a great way to clean up copper pennies and remove the patina from them as well.

7 Place the wet metal into a 1 gallon plastic bucket. It is now in a contained area where the sample can stay as wet as possible for as long as possible.

8 Add 2 ounces of ammonia to a smaller plastic cup. Ammonia is most commonly an active ingredient in household glass cleaners.

Accelerating the Rusting Process CONTINUED

9 Set the small cup of ammonia in the 1 gallon bucket, making sure the chemicals and containers are separate! The fumes alone will create the chemistry we're looking for in a safe and controlled manner.

10 Ammonia mixed directly with or poured onto the vinegar solution will make a toxic gas called chloramine that can be dangerous. There may already be a mix of odors present from the vinegar and ammonia. Make sure you're in a well-ventilated area when doing this experiment or anything similar. Stay safe!

11 To speed the process, use cellophane to place a temporary lid on the large bucket. You do not want a fully air-tight seal, just a way to contain the fumes.

12 A wrap of masking tape will hold the plastic in place while still allowing air to enter or escape the bucket. Wear safety glasses (not shown) and gloves! This allows you to look over into the bucket to see the process happen without being exposed to any fumes.

13 After only 5 minutes, you can see a noticeable change in the metal. A nice film of rust is forming on the metal surface.

14 We allowed our sample to sit in the covered bucket overnight. You can see the amazing (and quite beautiful) layer of rust that has formed over the metal. A few hours and basic chemistry has taken the place of years of natural deterioration.

Bleach, Vinegar, and Steel

Metal responds differently to bleach and to vinegar. With the two effects in mind, you have a variety of surfaces and effects to play with in your creation of fauxtina. When you think about it, to be able to create the illusion of steel that has sat in the elements for decades in the space of a couple of hours or weeks is powerful! When you consider that a typical paint job takes weeks to complete, or even months and years for some DIY painters, a few weeks to create a great-looking patina on steel is not much time at all!

To show the different effects that can be obtained, we did a bleach

Wearing a rubber glove for protection, I wet my hand with vinegar. For safety and contamination purposes, we always use gloves to perform experiments like this.

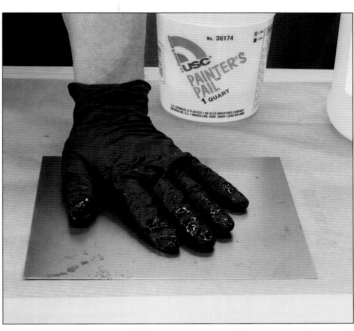

I then placed my hand flat against the 22-gauge untreated steel panel. This produces a wet impression of my hand on the panel.

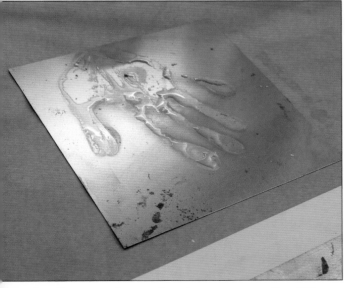

Seconds after removing my hand, you can see the difference between the dry metal and the effect of the vinegar on the metal. A slight halo of rust is already forming.

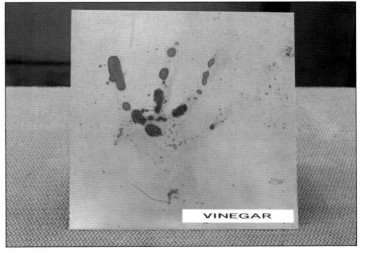

One month later, the effects of the vinegar are very clear. The acid has etched into the top layer of the metal panel and accelerated the oxidation process by quite a lot compared to the years it might usually take to create the same amount of corrosion.

We did the same process to a 22-gauge untreated steel panel using household bleach.

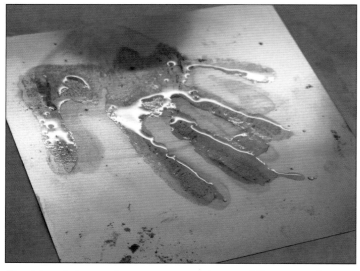

The bleach is much more aggressive, and it evaporates more slowly than the vinegar. A few minutes after contact, you can see the chemical reaction starting and the hand impression becoming very clear very fast!

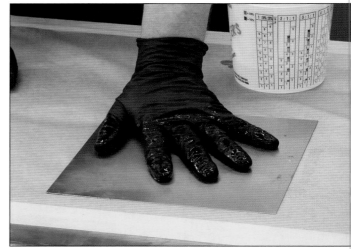

Again, I placed my hand flat against the panel, leaving a clear handprint on the surface.

One month later, the panel is aggressively corroding and rusting at a much faster rate than with the vinegar. Bleach is a natural oxidizing agent, which means that it adds oxygen molecules to the chemical process, facilitating rust even faster when exposed to the hydrogen (moisture) that in the air and atmosphere that we breathe. Notice also tha the rust extends past the handprint, which gives clues to the chemical process that affects the surrounding metal or a microscopic level, even outside the point of direct contac

versus vinegar experiment. It was done with the metal panels inside, in conditioned air, and not exposed to the outdoor elements. The process takes weeks instead of hours, but the results are truly authentic and genuinely oxidized.

Metallic Paint Systems

Creating the illusion of rust on a surface that doesn't typically rust is a bit of a challenge. Certainly technology has helped with that challenge in the past few years. There are now conductive primers tha can be sprayed on non-conductiv substrates, such as plastic, fiberglas glass, and even wood, which open up the opportunity to chrome plat many different surfaces by basicall fooling the electrostatic process int

Adhesion

Just like in an automotive paint job, you need to consider adhesion to the surface you are trying to patina. Primer requires sanding scratches to hang on to, so your base material (whatever it is) needs to be properly cleaned and sanded with a medium-grit paper or pad. It would be kind of disappointing to see the primer delaminate from your project and continue rusting on the floor. ■

The first step is to gather supplies. Our can has been sandblasted, so it has a rough surface for the paint to cling to. Scuffing the surface with 180-grit sandpaper will also help with adhesion. Also gather a chip brush, the oxidizing-iron primer, and a rust-activating spray.

participating in the chemistry of application.

In the chrome-plating process, there must be a cathode-anode positive and negative charge to deposit the layers that make up chrome finishes. There is a copper deposit followed by zinc then followed by chromium that gives it the luster that we've come to expect to see in chrome. It was impossible to electrostatically plate the different metals that make the layers of the chrome-plated finish.

There are now a number of craft and hobby paint and primer systems that are designed to transfer enough of an electrical charge to complete the process of plating and yield a very nice chrome-plated sur-face that wasn't previously possible. These paint systems contain iron (or other metal) that is suspended in liquid that will oxidize on its own over time due to the hydrogen and oxygen that naturally occurs in the air. There are several mild acid

The thick oxidizing paint can be brushed, blotted, or spray painted on with a good primer spray gun. We're using a chip brush so we can create some texture on the smooth surface of the can.

We applied a single coat since it went on thick with our brush. A second coat may be needed, depending on the surface and the application of the product.

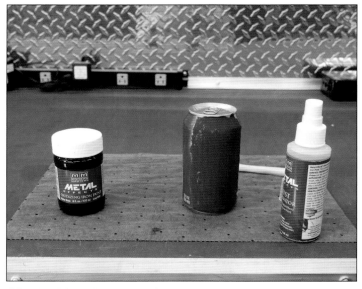

After waiting about 30 minutes, our surface was dry to the touch. This product will naturally rust if you simply leave it alone due to moisture in the air, but we wanted to use the accelerator to speed up the process.

An activator is a mild acid that reacts with the iron in the paint and the atmosphere. Two different rust activators are available for this paint: one that creates an orange rust and one that creates a greenish oxidation.

It only takes a single coat of activator to start rusting. Notice that I'm wearing gloves and know that I also have safety glasses on behind the camera! This is a mild acid spray, so care must be taken.

Immediately after spraying the paint, we started seeing a change to a rusty color. After 10 to 15 minutes, things really started to transform!

activators that give the metal in the primer a kick-start and begin the oxidation process instantly. They will create patina over nonconductive and even nonmetallic surfaces. You can easily achieve a traditionally rusty look or a green tarnished look similar to what occurs on copper by using the different metals in the primer and different activators in the paint system.

These paints are easy to use and can be purchased in kits that give a specific effect, including iron and copper patina. The beauty of a rusting paint system is that the patina is engineered into the paint itself and will give the same controlled effect regardless of what surface it's sitting on. This means that you can "rust" plastic, porcelain, rubber, vinyl, glass, aluminum, or any other surface that you can get paint to adhere to.

Due to the different thicknesses of the brush-coated rusting paint, the oxidation is uneven. In my eyes, the unevenness makes it more authentic looking. An hour's drying time gave us a timeworn look.

While we had our supplies out, we thought it might be fun to rust some wood! The unfinished wood is porous and takes the rusting paint on quickly and with good adhesion. Make sure the wood is clean and dry if you try this effect.

usting a Soda Can

Sometimes you want the look of sted iron, but you're working with material that is not iron and won't st, such as our aluminum soda n. To demonstrate how versatile d creative products like this can , we picked up this oxidizing iron int at a hobby store. The following quence shows how to create rust an aluminum can.

Sealing and Locking Down Patina

Sometimes you just want to stop e rusting process. Rust or patina can look so good and have so much character that you want to preserve it and keep that wonderful character that only time and nature can create. On a microscopic level, there are oxygen molecules that are trapped in the layer of rust, and there's no stopping that process, but it can be drastically slowed down to the point where we can't see it progress at all. There are a number of ways to lock out atmosphere from substrate, including clearcoats, phosphates, even products designed to lock down patina.

Locking down patina is done by simply starving the oxidation process from oxygen and hydrogen. It's like putting on a chemical Band-Aid. Eastwood makes a patina preserver spray that is a matte finish that is designed to protect the look of patina while drastically slowing the process of oxidation. There are also aerosol clearcoats in many forms, including catalyzed clear that is more of a permanent solution when wanting to bury your rust under a clear envelope. Be warned that spraying clearcoat onto a rusty panel can change the way it appears by changing the way light is reflected from the surface. A totally flat clear is your best bet if the paint is faded, but a satin or semigloss is a popular look as well.

Capturing the Natural Patina

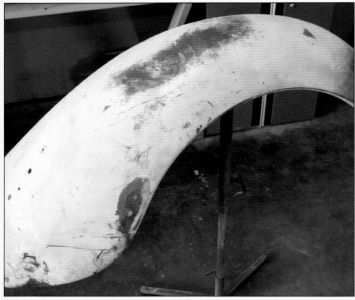

1 This is my favorite panel of the entire book! It's from a 1970 VW Bug, and it was donated by J3 restoration in Columbia, Tennessee, a shop that specializes in Volkswagen and Porsche restoring and preserving. I have spent many hours photographing old panels, parts cars, and restoration candidates at J3, and I have used these photos regularly as a reference to authentic patina.

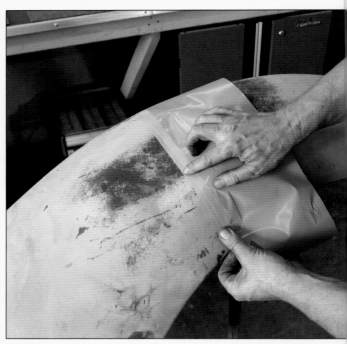

2 For our exercise, we masked off half of the zone we want to preserve. We did that so that we will have a reference point showing us whether the preserver change the color or appearance of the rust or if it maintains its wonderful character.

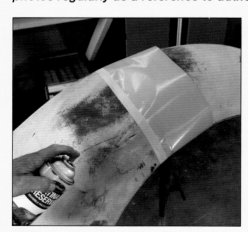

3 Two coats of Eastwood Patina Preserver were sprayed on the unmasked portion, waiting 5 minutes between coats. Allow the panel to dry for 10 minutes before removing any masking paper.

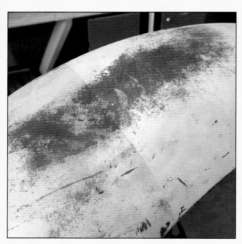

4 Although there is a slight difference in the two sides, the richness of the rust is still obvious and the color of the faded paint is very close to the uncoated side.

5 Eastwood 2K Aero-Spray is a professional catalyzed paint in an aerosol can that contains hardene in a separate chamber that is sealed until activated. Be aware of safety concerns with this product! Wear the required paint mask, gloves, and eye protection!

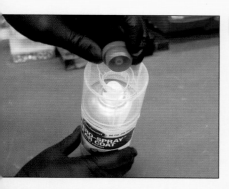

6 Remove the red button from the cap and invert the can to break the catalyst seal at the bottom.

7 Press the button onto the plunger on the bottom, then press it into the can to break the seal. This takes a little pressure, so make sure you hear the sound of the seal breaking.

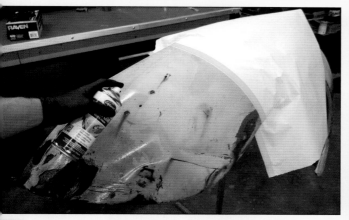

8 Apply two medium coats of the Eastwood 2K Aero-Spray matte clear with about 5 minutes waiting time between coats. Hold the can about 4 inches from the surface and use the standard 50-percent overlap for even application.

9 As the matte clear dries, it takes on less and less of a shine until it's almost completely flat after 20 to 30 minutes.

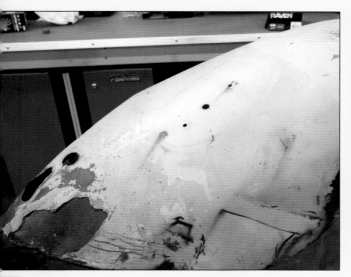

10 There is a very subtle sheen, and the color is slightly richer than the noncoated color.

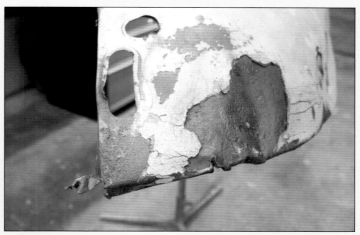

11 The rust still has a rich, oxidized color and has not lost any of its appeal. This product cures to a very hard surface and should almost eliminate the rust progressing any further.

Making New Plastic Look Old

Plastic has been a component of vehicle construction since the 1920s with Bakelite and cellulous materials. Plastic has evolved along with the automobile, and its use in vehicle construction has continued to rise.

Plastic, in any form, suffers from oxidation the same way steel does. The reaction between substrate and atmosphere causes oxidation, and eventually the plastic breaks down and deteriorates. Plastic degradation looks more like paint fading than metal rusting, but a distinct patina is apparent with most plastics that are a few years old.

Molded plastic typically has no protective coating, so the deterioration can happen quickly. As vehicles from the 1970s and 1980s a becoming popular "classics," repr duction parts are more and mo available. Mixing brand-new repr duction lights in with a patina pai job would look incorrect, so the cha lenge now is to create an authent look to reproduction plastics whi maintaining visibility and safe ope ation on the vehicle.

Aging Plastic

1 *This 1978 Camaro turn signal assembly is a new aftermarket part and looks great. If your goal is to restore a vehicle back to showroom condition, then your work is done once you take this out of the box. However, we want this to look as if it was original to the car and has aged in the sun for decades, so there's some strategy and technique involved.*

2 *Gather abrasives to style and age this part, startin with red, grey, and white scuffing pads. Each pad has a specific grit range: red is 220–400 grit, gray is 320–600 grit, white is 800–1000 grit. All three have specific roles in this project. The 220-grit sandpaper will be used as well.*

3 *Remove the bezel from the light housing on this two-piece assembly. That way, you can do a better job of styling.*

4 *Starting with the gray scuffing pad, knock the shin off the surface of the molded plastic. Gloss is not patina! Even fauxtina needs to look real, and gloss is on of the first appearances to go when parts age. Make sure you scuff all of the internal surfaces so no shiny spots emerge later.*

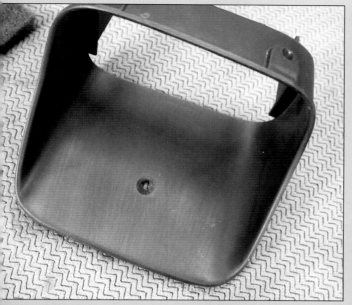

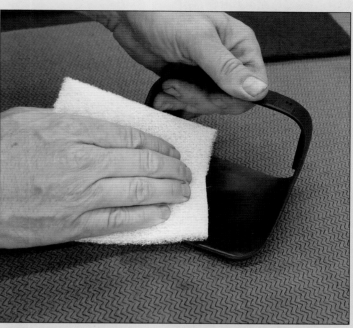

5 *Although the gloss is now muted, you can clearly see the scratch pattern from the scuffing pad in the plastic. This is more prevalent in plastic than it is in paint, so another step is needed on the ABS substrate than would have been necessary with a painted surface.*

6 *The white pad will help remove the scratch pattern left by the gray pad. It will actually buff a slight gloss into some of the raised areas of the bezel, giving an uneven matte finish to the part.*

7 *The signal light housing is next. Take time to remove the Z28 specific crossbar from the front of the lens. There are locating pins on either side, and you can simply push from behind the crossbar to separate the two pieces easily since there is an interference fit and no adhesive holding them together.*

8 *Starting with the gray pad and using a light touch, scuff the top surface of the plastic to dull the gloss and put a haze or diffusion onto the plastic. The gray pad puts a visible scratch into the surface, so a second step is required for this process.*

Aging Plastic *CONTINUED*

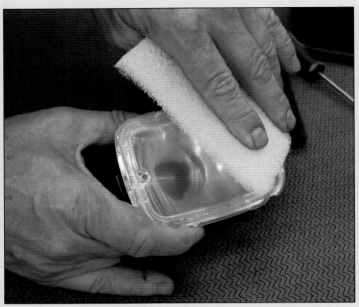

9 The white pad evens out the scratches and gives us the appearance of faded and oxidized plastic. The scuffed surface changes the way light is reflected back to your eyes, thereby changing the way we see the light.

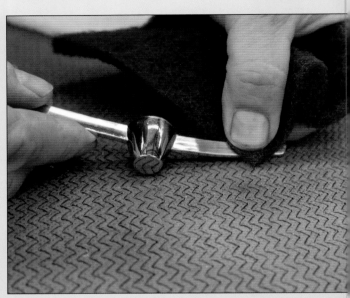

10 Next, style the Z28 crossbar, starting with the red scuffing pad. This part is made of plastic with plating that is very thin and weak due to the soft substrat that the chroming is on top of and the nature of the platin process on plastic.

11 Following the aggressive scratches of the red pad with gray will even out the surface and help make it look faded rather than sanded.

12 Looking closely at the surface reveals what happe to the edges when the 220-grit sandpaper is used on the corners. The black plastic substrate is exposed, making it look like the chrome has faded off over time.

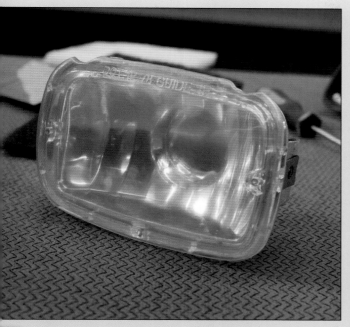

3 *Here you can see the benefit of scuffing the surface of the lens. You can also see that the reflective parabolic surface on the inside of the light is still new looking and very bright. It requires another process to remedy that.*

14 *Elmer's wood glue has a slightly yellowish cast to it, even when dry. This will give us a better aged look as well as a fuzzy and matte finish when the glue dries. Measure some wood glue into a small cap.*

5 *Add a drop of black craft paint into the glue to create a darker tint while still having a tan appearance when dry. These products need to be mixed thoroughly before application.*

16 *A very small amount is all that's needed here, so we're mixing this into a lid with a modeling brush. The acrylic craft paint adds strength to the water-based glue, giving it a more permanent effect.*

Aging Plastic CONTINUED

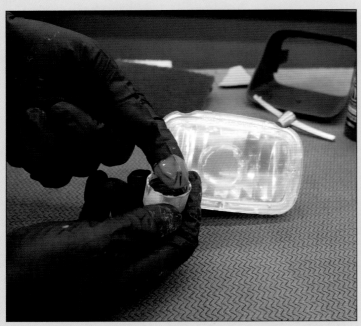

17 You can see the translucent quality of this mix. It is applied with the gloved fingertip inserted into the bulb opening at the back of the light.

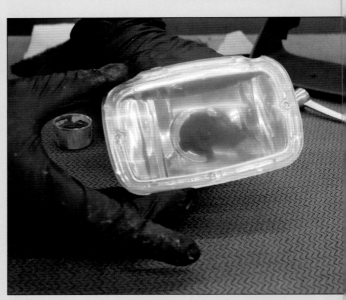

18 Although it's difficult to see due to the hazy lens, using your fingertip to carefully apply the mix to th shiny reflective surface without getting any on the inside of the lens is important! Take your time and work slowly and carefully.

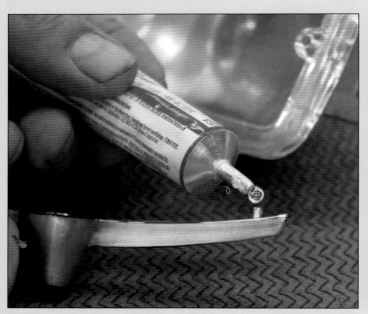

19 While the parabolic dries, which should take 10 to 15 minutes in normal temperatures, glue the crossbar back in place on the lens. Use model builders glue carefully applied to the locating pins of the bar.

20 You will start seeing the big picture on this piece when you look at everything at this stage. You will also see that you may not be able to properly fade the ler surface with the crossbar in place.

1 The finished and assembled turn signal looks much different, and obviously much more fatigued by time than it did moments ago. Details like this on every aspect of a vehicle will lend authenticity to your patina job. It's truly the details that count with fauxtina!

Distressing Glass

New glass allows light to pass through with little refraction and minimal disturbance. This provides few distractions and gives us a pleasing feeling when we look through clean and clear glass. As glass gets old and worn, the surfaces take on a diffusing quality, drawing our attention to small defects and damage. It can even cause fatigue when driving due to the divided focus from the driver's perspective.

Glass shows wear in different ways. It can develop chips, abrasions, scratches, fading, wiper scrub marks, and, in the case of laminated glass, air bubbles forming as the two panes separate from the plastic film between them. Vehicle manufacturers transitioned from laminated side glass to tempered safety glass in the early to mid 1950s. Laminated side glass was a sheet of thin plastic sandwiched in between two panes of plate glass that had the function of holding the sharp shards of broken glass together and hopefully away from passengers in the event of a collision. Although somewhat safer than shattered plate glass in an accident, the laminated glass was quite dangerous if a passenger came in contact with damaged or broken panes. The department of transportation mandated transition from laminated glass to tempered glass that would shatter into tiny (less harmful) pieces of glass if broken.

As laminated glass deteriorates and separates, it has a distinctive

This is the passenger vent glass from a 1956 Ford. This car was obviously made before the change to tempered glass on the side windows. Ford was a leader in safety innovations, being the first manufacturer to move the ignition key out of the line of impact from the driver as well as the first to have a standard-issue dash pad on all vehicles from 1955 on. Our intent is not to deceive an observer as to what year the vehicle was made, rather to create an authentic patina down to the last details of the glass. This side glass will serve as our guide while styling our new pane of tempered glass.

look that can be a signature to a time period. The edges of the laminated panes allow moisture and air to creep between the laminated plastic and glass over time, and since the plastic has limited UV protection on the edges, they would yellow and discolor after years of exposure. Glass can be particularly difficult to patinize due to its hardness and lack of porosity, which makes it difficult for coatings to adhere. One of the options to create adhesion and show age is to use abrasion techniques, but be forewarned that any abrasive technique can be extremely difficult to reverse.

Creating Aged Glass

The methods in this project are best tried out on a practice pane first. Don't ever make your project t subject of research! Know what y want to do before you commit your project. We're starting out wi a brand-new vent glass from a C truck from a popular aftermarket c alog vendor. Ours is removed fro the framework and from the ve cle, but all of the steps can be do with the window in the vehicle an mounted in its normal location.

Creating Aged Glass

1 Our glass-distressing project begins with a brand-new aftermarket vent glass from a C10 truck. This pane is tempered glass, and similar panes are available from a number of aftermarket vendors. Replacement glass can be expensive, so experiment on a test piece first.

2 The first step is to use a dual-action sander with fine 600-grit sandpaper that is attached to a soft interface pad. The glass surface is very hard, and it will take some time for abrasion to show up like we want it to Have patience with these steps.

3 Lightly pressing on the surface of the glass, keep the sander moving evenly over the entire surface s the sanding marks will be as even as possible over the whole piece of glass. You'll start to see a slight haziness after a few minutes. Resist the urge to sand until it's dull. You're trying to fade the surface, not prep it for paint!

4 The next step is to sand the scratched surface with 1500-grit sandpaper. This will give another dimension to the faded appearance, as well as remove some of the curved scratches made by the action of the oscillating sanding pad.

5 The 1500-grit sandpaper is very fine, and it will take some time to show any effect on the glass. Take your time, stop and check your progress several times, and have your sample piece close by to compare your actual project to.

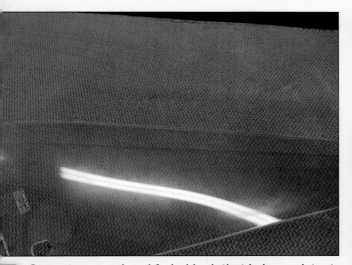

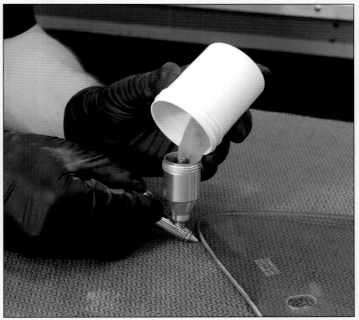

6 Stop at an aged and faded look that is inconsistent and quite authentic to your eyes. The next stage of this project involves "smoking" the edge of the vent glass, as is commonly found on vintage vehicles. This is done with a detail-etching airbrush. These can be found in hobby stores and online for a reasonable price. Typically, this tool is used for etching logos or designs into glass, but in our case, we're etching a fade into the edge.

7 An ultrafine abrasive dust is loaded into the tank of the etching airbrush. It's important to use a very fine media with this project so you have the appearance of a gradual fade and not a pitted or sandblasted surface.

Creating Aged Glass CONTINUED

8 I'm using an airbrush compressor that puts out 5 to 8 psi, which is perfect for this project. You can use any compressed-air source, but you must regulate it down to a very low pressure so that you have the most control possible. There's no going back with these steps.

9 Stay an inch or so away from the surface so that th' pattern of the media on the glass is wide and subtle. Moving in closer will make a more consistent line on the glass and is not what we're after on this project. W want a timeworn and gradual look to this edge.

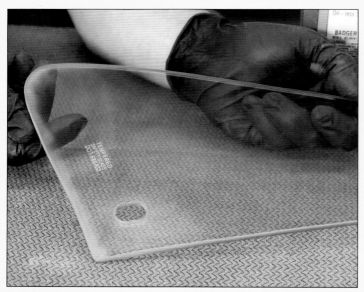

10 Notice that we're not fogging the entire edge of the glass. This is because we want to mimic the authentic fading that usually only happens on the lower edges of these vent glasses.

11 The final technique on this project is to mimic a laminated glass panel. Our goal is to give an appearance of vintage glass but still retain the safety of a modern tempered glass. We're using a modeling glue placed on the back side of the glass to create the effect of delamination between the layers of safety glass and the plastic middle layer.

2 Keeping tight to the lower edge, apply small blobs of glue in a random line along the edge.

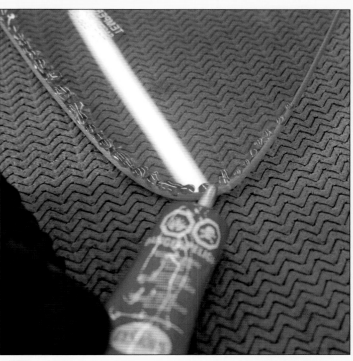

13 Just like the fogged edge, we're staying with the lower forward edge of the glass for realism.

4 The final detail is to create a stain on the delamination effect. An airbrush with rust-colored paint carefully applied will work well, but a highlighter pen gave us the yellowed look we wanted to see that matched a vintage piece of glass we found in our travels.

15 Looking through the exterior side of the glass, we have a faded window with a dirty, fogged lower portion. The added effect of delaminating dual-layered glass created an authentic look to this brand-new piece of vent window glass.

*U*SING THE *A*IRBRUSH

The airbrush is a tool that has played a major role in the evolution of automotive artwork over the past several decades. It is incredibly versatile, giving you the ability to dispense paint in a very controlled and detailed manner. Much like a typical paint spray gun, the airbrush blends a supplied air source with paint in a valve to create droplets, or atomized paint particles, that are carefully blown onto a panel or subject.

The first known origins of airbrush art are actually cave drawings created by pigment blown through reeds and cupped hands to create shading, shadows, and fine detail in stone-aged imagery and art. Before the digital artwork that is so prevalent in our world today, airbrush was used heavily in advertising fine art. The first patent on an airbrush was granted in 1876 by Francis Edgar Stanley (famous for the Stan- ley Steamer), but there is no know surviving art that was done with th device. The airbrush paved the wa for the invention of the modern spra gun, showing that paint delivery w much more efficient if atomize This technology has revolutionize the refinish industry worldwide ar changed the way vehicles, amor other products, are painted. Toda it has become a staple in the custo painting world.

Airbrush art and custom ai brushing on vehicles goes in and o of vogue, but the ability to crea detailed murals and realistic art is valuable skill that takes years to ma ter. However, the tool is essential very simple and can be used with very basic knowledge of the wor ings. We use the airbrush for patir in a number or ways, primari enhancing the look of corrosion, cr ating water stains, perfecting fade lines, and creating subtle effects tha can't be achieved with larger equi ment or brushes.

Types of Airbrushes

There are two types of airbrushe single action and dual action. Sing action is simpler to operate but giv

Airbrushing doesn't have to be intimidating. It's actually fun!

ou less control of the spray pattern nd dispersion of paint. Dual action ves you more precise control over ne paint pattern but is slightly more ifficult to master. It's very similar to elding. The MIG welder only has to orry about settings on the machine nd proper technique; he or she mply pulls the trigger and the pro- ss happens as long as the trigger is ulled and the welding wand is close the metal work surface. A TIG elder must have tighter tolerances n the metal, a finer level of fabrica- on, and a clearer understanding of e substrate being worked on. He she must control the heat with a ot pedal, feed metal by hand with eehand tig rods, and control the ngsten wand. The end result from e commitment of learning the dis- pline and perfecting the skill of TIG elding, much like a dual-action air- ush, is finer control and the ability perform more-detailed work.

You don't need to have much xperience to use an airbrush. A basic nderstanding of the equipment and little practice will get you familiar lough with the airbrush to create mple fading effects. Over time, ur confidence will rise alongside ur skill. You can create fantastic fects by simply shading colors on panel, which comes in particularly andy while creating patina.

To tell the truth, most airbrush t is done almost completely with encils and mask techniques; very w professional airbrush artists use eehand techniques exclusively. A rofessional has a great degree of ill involved and a masterful control ver the airbrush as well as the ability freehand some of his work, but the ending of stencils, using masking chniques for sharp lines and shad- g, and advanced freehand skills are

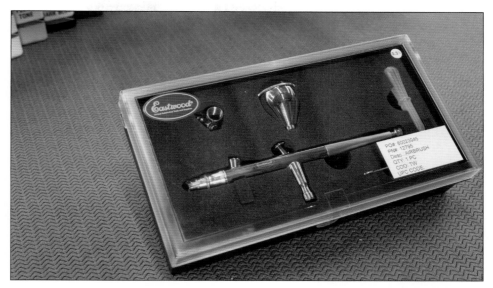

This dual-action airbrush is from the Eastwood Company. It's a gravity-fed brush with a tank on top that is easy to fill and clean. The dual action is in the trigger, which gives you much more control over the spray pattern. Even though it's a little more complicated to learn this style of brush, you'll catch on quickly. The brush is disassembled in the box, which doubles as a great storage case.

the result of years of practice.

A dual-action airbrush is a ver- satile tool with many options for precisely applying paint. There are many brands and styles of airbrush, and it's subjective as to which will work best for your project. Once you decide what style of brush you want, don't be afraid to experiment with it and see if there are alternative tech- niques you can find. Most custom painters are unafraid of breaking the rules, and that comes with the confi- dence gained from experience.

Tools for Airbrushing

There are many different brands of airbrushes to choose from with varying price points. Instead of recom- mending a brand, I'm recommend- ing a style of brush: the gravity-fed brush with a removable top. This seems to be the most user-friendly design that is easy to clean and main- tain. It's also a dual-action airbrush

that gives you much more control over the fluid coming out the end. Although it's a little more difficult to learn, the techniques will give you much more versatility, even as a nov- ice. A single-action airbrush is less expensive to buy and easier to use, but it's worth a little more cash and a little more time to learn with dual action.

There are several other tools that are helpful to have around:

- Paint cup and cap
- Wrench for disassembly and assembly
- Protective cover for the brush air cap
- Dropper
- Push-style air fitting
- Compressed air source
- Standard airbrush air hose
- Regulator
- Airbrush workstation
- Inline moisture filter

This dual-action airbrush came with an adapter for a push-style air hose, the paint cup and cap, a wrench for disassembly and assembly, a protective cover for the brush air cap, and a dropper for adding small amounts of paint to the cup.

The paint cup has a cap that is a compression fit, which means it doesn't have threads. This fits snugly and is easy to remove without threads, which makes it convenient to remove to add paint or tint colors.

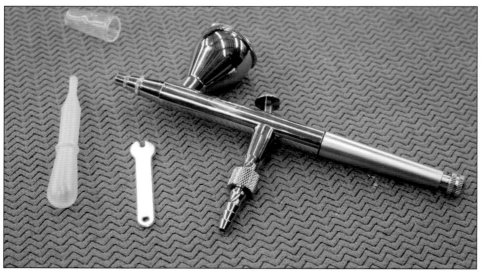

The push-style air fitting is nice to have if you don't have a conventional air supply. You can use any number of compressed air sources and a simple Tyvek hose, or a rubber hose pushed onto the fitting, to power the brush.

There are many different hose configurations, but this one a standard airbrush air hose. It has one end that has /8-inch female threads to fit the airbrush and the other as 1/2-inch female threads that are standard in air hose ttings with large and small guns. There are many different dapters available as well that can reduce or increase your onnection size to your air source.

If you're using a conventional air compressor, or even a portable air tank with 5/16 ID fittings, you'll need to use a regulator because the airbrush only requires low air pressure at the gun inlet (8 to 20 psi, depending on the material and goals).

Our Badger electric air compressor is a workhorse, and it will serve us very well for all of our needs. It has a maximum working pressure of 28 psi, but we can regulate that down easily if we need to. These compressors need no maintenance, but after some time can run hot. They may require a water separator of some sort to keep moisture out of your paint and project.

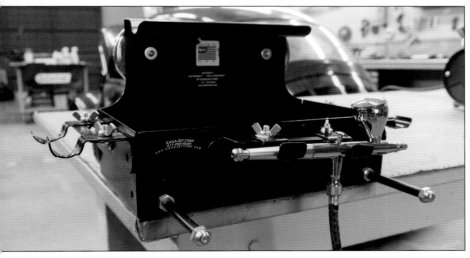

Although not a necessity, this Karajen Corp Airport airbrush workstation is nice to have as a gun holder. It features several brush-holding fixtures, a storage compartment, and pins to hang your air hose on.

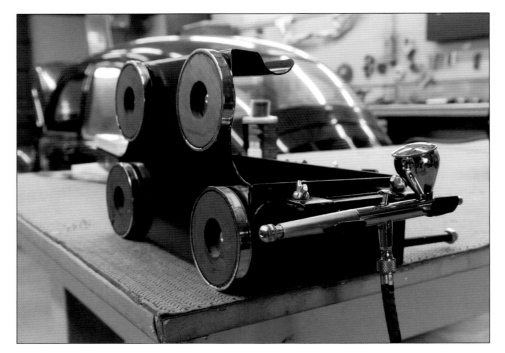

The best feature of the Karajen workstation is the magnetic mounting solution. It's superconvenient to be able to mount the workstation to any metal surface, and our roll-around tool carts will serve as our temporary staging area for our projects.

Here is our complete setup, which is very simple: just a brush, a hose, and a compressor. For most of our work, we'll use the unregulated PSI setting on the compressor of about 26 to 28 psi.

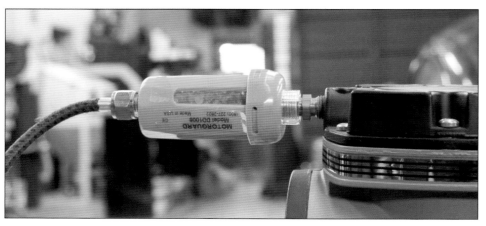

This is an inline moisture filter, which is designed to collect moisture in your airline from the compressor and not affect PSI output from the compressor. It's filled with desiccant spheres that will change to a blueish color when they're saturated with moisture. At that point, we'll just throw it away and install another.

Safety Equipment

We recommend that you always use safety equipment with atomized paints, regardless of the chemistry. Protecting your respiratory system is very important, so wear a mask or respirator when spraying paint. You should also wear gloves to protect from skin absorption. Solvent-based paint is impossible to remove with regular hand soap and difficult to clean with harsh soaps and chemicals, so the best way to keep your hands clean is to wear gloves whenever you're using solvent-based paint. The chemicals in the paint can get absorbed into your kidneys and liver very quickly and over time can cause health problems. Any time you're using paint materials, always read the safety recommendations from the manufacturers. There's valuable information that you need to know and understand. Avoid the risks and take the time to use the proper safety equipment. ■

We're using Inspire Paints on our projects. We got the base kit, which has a nice color selection including flesh tones. Some of the kit's dark oranges will make it easy for us to come up with a rusty color. We also got some of the Inspire reducer, so we can dilute the color strength of our colors. Making the colors thinner can help an inexperienced user by making mistakes less obvious, which is a nice feature.

Paint

There are two types of paint: water based or solvent based. Whichever you use is subjective, although many airbrush artists use water-based paints. T-shirt artists have traditionally used acrylic paints for creating their art, mostly because there are premixed colors available that are vivid and exciting right out of the bottle. The fumes and overspray from waterborne or water-based paints are less dangerous as well.

For the exercises in this chapter, we're using a solvent-based system from Inspire Paints. Inspire paints are solvent based and offer many specialty colors and effects. We are using the base kit from Inspire that is compatible with our topcoat system on the main project. The base kit includes 10 premixed colors, so all you need to do is shake them up and shoot them.

Airbrush Techniques

Practice is the key to mastering any art form, and it's also the way to become comfortable enough to accomplish a particular project goal.

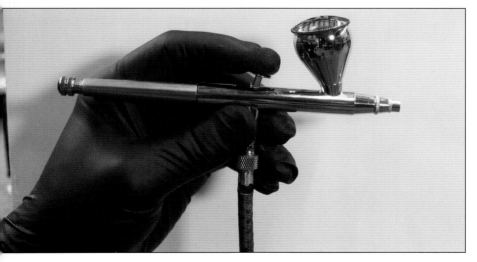

The basic hand position of any airbrush is to hold it as you do a pencil. The tip faces away from you. You'll notice we're wearing gloves since we're using solvent-based airbrush paint.

The trigger action in particular has to be learned. Once you train your muscle memory on how the trigger dispenses paint and air, you'll be able to spray without thinking about it. That's when you will get great results from your airbrush.

We're going to show you some basic exercises with a dual-action airbrush. The exercises are simple and fun, and they will give you a starting point to produce great results with limited knowledge of the equipment. Use these fundamentals to build your skills and become a talented airbrush artist.

Our easel for these exercises is a peel-away sheet board that is made for polyester fillers to be mixed o then thrown away, revealing a ne clean sheet every time. These shee have been developed for the aut body industry as a convenient an stable mixing palate for polyester fil ers. These opinion boards work pe fectly for our practice sessions wit the airbrush.

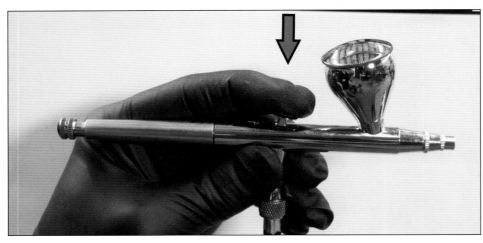

A dual-action airbrush trigger has tw functions. The first is to allow air to move through the brush to be mixed with paint at the fluid tip. This action is done by pressing straight down on the spring-loaded trigger. As you press downward, more air is release into the path of air and paint, giving you detailed control.

The second action of the dual-action airbrush is to introduce paint to the airstream by pulling the trigger back ward while holding it down. The mor you pull backward, the more paint is allowed into the airstream.

The fluid adjustment knob at the end of this Eastwood brush is a very nice feature. You can preset your fluid delivery at various amounts, which allows you to focus on differen aspects of painting without worrying about using too much paint. This comes in handy when creating shad- ows or subtle effects that have to be carefully painted on.

Dots

1 We're going to show you some practice exercises to get you ~~sed~~ to the basic operations of the ~~ual~~-action brush. We'll start with ~~'ack~~ paint on a white background. ~~ne~~ of the nice things about Inspire ~~aints~~ is that you only have the shake ~~em~~ up before using, no mixing! ~~ey're~~ ready to spray.

2 Gently push the air control downward and ease it back about half way. This makes a dot. Dots teach good trigger control.

3 Practice making dots the same size, then pull the airbrush back farther away from the panel. The dots get bigger, but the edges also get fuzzier and softer. It almost looks as if the image is out of focus, but this is because the overspray is so gradual around the edges of the circle.

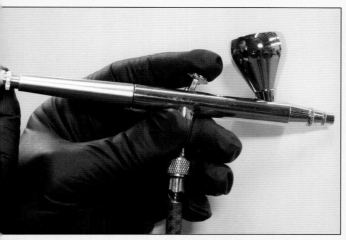

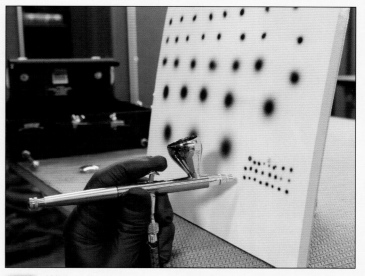

4 Once you're comfortable with dots of different sizes and seeing how the proximity of the airbrush to the ~~anel~~ changes the dot size and sharpness of the edges, ~~√~~ adjusting down the fluid control at the end of the brush. ~~irning~~ this to the right restricts the amount of paint that ~~ets~~ pushed through the fluid tip and gives you more control.

5 With a limited amount of paint moving through the tip, you can get much closer to the panel. The paint is carefully dispensed, allowing you to make much smaller dots and have more control over the process.

Lines and Fill

1 Your next exercise is making lines on the page. Start moving the airbrush and feed in the paint, keeping the brush moving as you let off the trigger. This keeps your ends tapered and smooth instead of flooded out at each end, which is called feathering.

2 Once you're comfortable with your lines, and the beginning and ending is smooth on each one, you can start to create a fill pattern. This is done by overlapping each line by 50 percent and slowly filling in the space. This technique is important to master if you need to cover large areas evenly.

3 Be very careful while attempting this exercise! The paint is less diffused when you remove the cap, and you can produce much more precise lines and detail, but there's risk! If you bend the needle on your brush, it's nearly impossible to straighten it, and a bent needle basically ruins the function of your airbrush. If you try these techniques, please be careful with your needle.

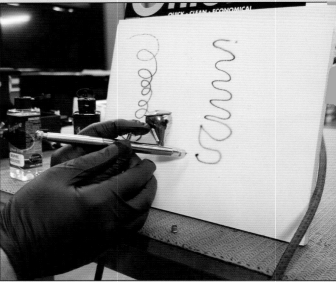

4 Remove the end-cap and practice making much smaller lines with more precision. Pay close attention to how close you are to the panel. Increase your air pressure and back off the fluid control to create an even tighter and smaller line.

Stippling and Other Effects

Stippling is a neat effect that can give you everything from a random-splatter look to a granite-textured look. Using a stippling technique with a rusting primer can yield interesting results on almost any substrate! You could create the appearance of bubbled and rusting chrome or pitted rust on something that would never rust.

Making Rust Color

Rust is the color of, well, rust! It's an oxide red, which ironically is the color of some primers that are formulated to protect metal from rust, so it's not a difficult color to create. The airbrush allows you to use shading, fading, and stippling to give the appearance of realistic rust.

Stippling is a neat way to create random splatters on a panel. Jackson Pollock did it by dripping paint off of brushes and other items, but we can stipple with the airbrush and a wood paddle to create interesting droplet sizes.

Creating a rust-streak effect is basically making a dot and combining that with a line that tapers off. Practicing this will teach you great trigger control!

Here's the actual bottom line: Just mess around! Figure out what the brush can do, and it will tell you what you need to practice with. Templates are great fun to work with as well; experiment with them too! But be free to just have fun with this amazing tool, and it will teach you how to use it.

Use the Inspire Paints to make a rusty brown color. You can use the exercises in chapter 5 to make colors with the help of a color wheel and basic color theory.

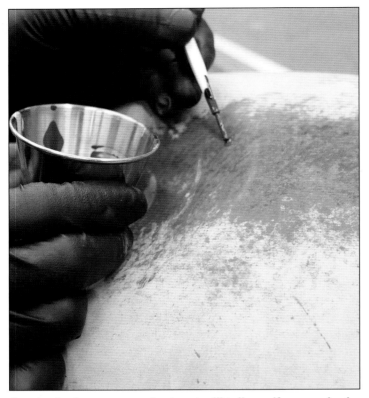

A color test on some actual rust will tell you if your color is close. This one looks exactly like the rusted pigment.

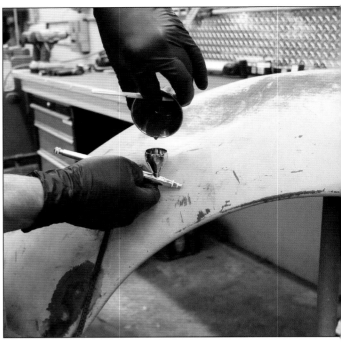

Here's where it helps to make notes! If we kept track of how many drops of each color it took to make our rust color, we could have a repeatable formula. While it is fun to experiment, it doesn't give us any information to guide us in order to remix when we run out of paint. Make sure you pay attention to your color experiments!

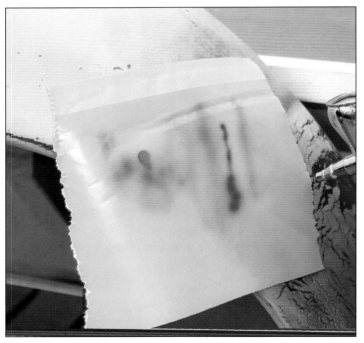

Never experiment on your panel! Always have a scrap sheet or paper to test your pattern and color on that's close to your work. Ours is a piece of masking paper taped to the other side of the fender.

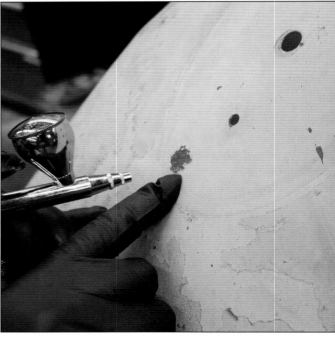

Here's our beautiful rusty spot that we're going to enhan with a water stain. This is actual rust, but we can make it much more dramatic if we are smart.

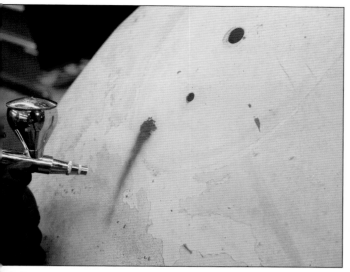

This is an easy effect to make, and it tells the story of a lot of moisture dragging the rust down over the paint. This is a combination of fauxtina and actual rust.

We're just randomly finding places that could benefit from streaks and styling them. This fender is a throwaway part, but was a lot of fun to practice on as well as a teaching tool that we can learn from.

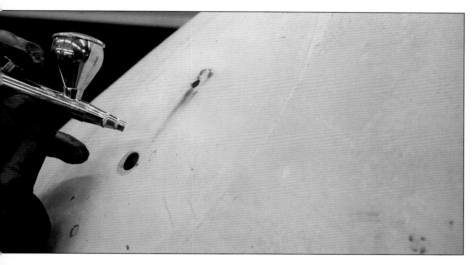

Here we are paying attention to light and gravity. Gravity will pull rust downward. By following this basic assumption of gravity, we can create authentic patina easily!

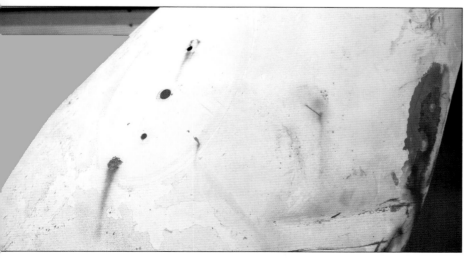

Creating patina is not about over-doing the effect, it's about making it authentic. Subtle details that are pur-posely created are the key to creating believable and attractive fauxtina.

VINTAGE SIGN PAINTING AND USING STENCILS

Commercial lettering and sign painting was once a popular art form that played a major role in local advertising. Hand-painted signs were certainly not exclusive to vehicles, but this commercialized art form and trade was a major part of vehicle commercial advertisement.

In the 1980s, digital graphics technology took over sign painting for everything from real estate companies to storefronts, glass, and even vehicle graphics, nearly killing off the entire hand-painting industry. Recently there has been a nostalgic comeback of sorts that has given a nod toward hand-lettering skills, but the trade and industry as a whole will never be wh[...] it once was.

There has always been a cult-li[...] following of traditional pinstripe[...] in the hot rod industry that specia[...] ize in period-correct artwork. Th[...] niche art form stems from the orig[...] nal coachbuilders and sign painter[...] The custom painting communi[...] has always embraced the art form [...] "pulling lines" on old cars as a way [...] finalize and to finish airbrushed a[...] work or restoration-style accent a[...] enhancement.

There are artists who still car[...] the torch of the old trades and car[...] forward the skills they've acquire[...] during decades of striping. Rick Ha[...] ris from Nashville, Tennesse, studi[...] under Shakey Jake, who was mentor[...] by the legendary Von Dutch (Kenne[...] Howard). Harris currently teach[...] classes on the art of pinstriping a[...] sign painting, offering a blend of tr[...] ditional and original styles and tec[...] nology. To create the look of a faded [...] badly worn sign that was hand-letter[...] many years ago is an art form, b[...] there are techniques using mode[...]

A popular trend in the fauxtina world is vintage sign painting. Trucks of the 1930s and 1940s were work vehicles, and lettered signs on doors and tailgates were a great source of advertisement for local businesses. This truck has a wonderful blend of new and old paint, including the sign and saw image.

supplies that will allow you to create the illusion of vintage aged lettering. There is a little more to it than simply sanding the letters to make them look faded (although that is certainly one of the ways to create the illusion of UV damage on decades-old materials). It's always fun to see what others have done, and to use that for inspiration or to steer clear of a method that you don't like.

You don't need to have dedicated 10 years of your life, or even a few weeks of your time to the discipline of hand lettering. We'll show you some easy techniques that require patience and some simple rules to be followed. Using modern stencils, some traditional paintbrushes, and striping materials combined with off-the-shelf paint supplies, you can create a wonderful patina effect on your project. The ability to sand through, fade out the letters, and create inconsistent lines adds to the aged look make it easy to create a faded and thin letter style without having a decade's worth of skill to paint it and several decades more for the lettering to deteriorate. Adding a vintage sign to an already-aged vehicle is common, and a great way to advertise a small business. It's an even more interesting way to personalize your vehicle if you're leaning toward an antique style.

Getting Ready

To practice creating vintage signage, we're going create a door sign with the name "Last Chance Garage" and a design in the middle. We will be using aerosol spray paint for the letters themselves in a drab-looking color that we hope looks period correct on the 1960s-era truck door. We'll also use 1-Shot striping paint and traditional camel hair striping brushes for

This Vintage Racing sign looks like it was hand-lettered many years ago, although this job was finished a few months prior to taking this photo. There's a faded white letter with a neutral gray drop shadow underneath for dimension. The painter used a wide lettering brush, and you can see the brushstrokes through the faded paint, lending an authentic look. Although the red paint on the truck is original, the lettering is not, providing a great blend of patina and fauxtina on this vehicle. The large rust patch where the paint is missing is a nice touch of authenticity as well.

accents and outlines. If you've never held a pinstriping brush before, don't worry! We're going to assume that you haven't and still show you how to get great results.

Supplies Needed

The specialty striping paints and brushes can be purchased through companies such as Eastwood, Autobody Toolmart, or other automotive specific outlets that cater to custom painting. The color palate of 1-Shot

lettering paint is vast! Colors are easy to blend together as well, so you can mix your own tones. We'll show you some basic palating (brush loading) techniques and how to make some simple lines on a panel. Practice is fun with these materials, and it is absolutely required.

Sanding through layers is a common theme with patina-creating methods, so it's no surprise that sandpaper is required with this project. We will use 1000 grit as well as 400 grit

We'll be spraying paint with this project: some with spray cans and some with a large spray gun. Always protect your respiratory system and work in a well-ventilated area. Gloves will protect from skin absorption, and glasses will protect your eyes from overspray or any splash risk.

The spray can and lacquer paint dries very quickly, so there's no need to cover the entire vehicle. We are, however, protecting the paint well past our project panel.

These self-adhesive stencils are thick, flexible, and have a low-tac adhesive that is easily reusable. Each letter is independent, and there were several fonts available. We were looking for a style that resembled a hand-lettered style, as well as more of a block-letter style.

for different techniques. We'll also use a gray scuffing pad, which is in the 400- to 600-grit range, that is perfect for putting enough scratch into the surface so that paint adheres without removing much paint material in the process.

There are supplies, tools, and safety equipment that you're going to need to do this project. First, basic safety equipment is always mandatory. If you're spraying paint, use respiratory protection. Gloves will protect your hands from messes and from chemical absorption. Safety glasses will prevent any kind of eye damage from splashes of paint, cleaners, or paint overspray.

To protect the body of the truck, we masked around the door wit 24-inch automotive masking pape and then further covered the pane with drop cloths. If you don't hav autobody supplies in your shop drop cloths, masking tape, and mask ing paper from a home center wi be cost-effective protection for you project.

For our large panels, we'll use high-volume, low-pressure (HVLI gun simply because it gives you mor even coverage, which is important fc the ground coat under our letterin project. You'll need an air compres sor with at least a 30-gallon air tan to spray a large project. For an all-ove paint job, you need more power an capacity, but since we're only sprayin one single panel here, a smaller size fine. There are electric turbine spra systems available as well, but if you'r going to be doing automotive refinisl ing projects, you'll need to invest i good quality air delivery component:

We're doing basic script and bloc lettering on a somewhat flat pane Stencils work well, but for this proje(self-adhesive stencils work extremel well! We found ours on the interne by doing a simple search using the siz

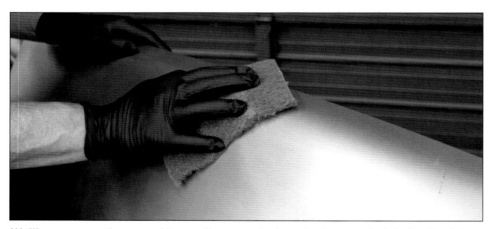

We'll use a practice panel to confirm our design strategy and style for the letters. This fender is painted with a matte finish green color that we'll treat as if it were original patina or vintage paint. This way we can create a paint strategy that we can duplicate on the project truck and get much more consistent and predictable results on our actual project. We're scuffing the surface for adhesion. The gray scuffing pads will scratch the surface without removing any of the paint, which is important for preserving existing patina. This is a practice session for the door of the project truck and will teach us how to ensure adhesion while maintaining the surface character.

After scuffing, clean any residue or dust off the surface with an aerosol glass cleaner. This cleaner contains no ammonia, and it is a good choice for prepainting surface prep.

A matte-clear spray is used to protect the patina of our subject. Spray cans are fine for this purpose, but use good technique and many medium-wet coats rather than full-wet coats. This will help the finish dry faster as well as build up evenly.

d basic style of lettering we want to e. There are many styles and sizes to oose from, but we thought that a nch letter size was adequate, and we ose a block-style letter along with a ndwriting-styled stencil. This gives a variety of letter styles that are eas- transferred. I avoid using the blocks stencils that are all connected on e sheet and those that have a por- n of the letter obstructed. We're try- g to resemble hand lettering, and we ed as complete a letter and charac- r profile as possible.

Create the Test Design

Before we go straight to the project, it's always a good idea to create a practice panel and test color choices and techniques. This late-model fender is painted with a matte-finish green color that's been recently applied, but our project vehicle (behind the fender) has its original paint that is in wonderfully horrible condition, and we want to make our sign match the style and age of the truck.

Our project is to create a "shop truck" sign on the door of this wonderfully horrible 1971 C10 truck. We'll match the original patina of the rest of the vehicle using the same techniques as our practice panel. Applying the ground coat of matte clear can be nice way of arresting the progress of time and preserving the patina. Keep in mind that there is a chemical process in play, and the rust will continue, although at a much slower rate than if it were left uncovered.

Preparing the Truck

1 While allowing the fender ground coat to dry, prep the main project. The door of our 1971 C10 truck has a nice mix of original paint and surface rust that is contributing to the crusty appearance overall.

2 The gray pads are fine enough to provide tooth to the topcoat of paint while leaving a fine scratch that will be undetectable under the protective layer of clear. Scuff the surface of your panel.

3 After scuffing the surface thoroughly, use an aerosol glass cleaner and a shop towel to clean the dust and any other debris off of the surface before masking.

4 Even though the paint on our truck is in terrible condition, the glass, wheels, and mirrors don't need paint overspray on them, so we're masking the area surrounding our painting zone to keep the contamination low.

5 You'll notice the color of the masking tape is not blue. The blue tape is for masking water-based paints, and we'll be using solvent paint. The backing paper and adhesive won't stand up to the solvents in the automotive paint, and will separate and leak. Make sure you use the correct masking tape for the paint you're using.

Applying the Clear

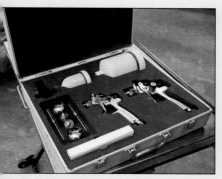

1 *Our HVLP spray gun kit comes from Eastwood. It has a 1.3-mm fluid tip with the larger gun, which makes it perfect for spraying full panels. There is also a small gun for detail spraying, as well as two different fluid tips for the large gun designed for spraying primers and thicker materials, making this a very versatile gun set.*

2 *We're using an off-the-shelf matte finish clearcoat that we picked up at a local auto parts store. This is a lacquer paint that does not require a catalyst, which makes it safer to spray.*

3 *After stirring the clearcoat thoroughly, always use a strainer to pour your paint through into the gun cup.*

4 *Check your pattern on the gun off to the side of the project. Masking paper is a perfect place to test. With the gun set fully open on every setting and at around 20 psi at the inlet, you should see an elongated elliptical shape (a stretched football).*

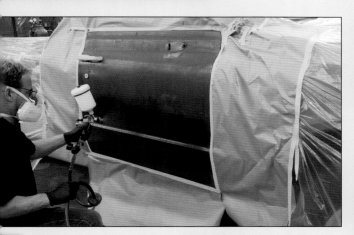

5 *Wear a good respirator, safety glasses, and gloves. Hold the gun about 6 inches off the panel and make even passes, overlapping each pass by 50 percent for even coverage on the door.*

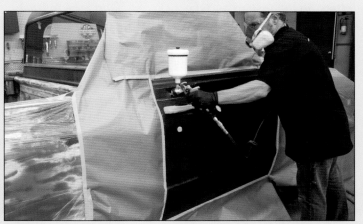

6 *Apply two full coats of clear on the panel. This will give adequate protection of the natural patina so you don't sand through it while trying to style the letters and sign.*

Spray Equipment Tips

When you're using automotive spray equipment, there are a few things you should remember and some habits you should have every time you spray. Our shop is well ventilated, and we're filtering the air coming in and out of the shop, which makes a nice cross flow of air. We're also using a non-catalyzed paint system, which is safer to use and dries much faster on the panels. Make sure you have at least a 5-hp compressor pump and at least 60 gallons of air storage if you're going to spray an all-over paint job. You can get away with smaller equipment on smaller projects, but proper air supply is critical to a good outcome when using this type of equipment. For most of this project, we're using aerosol paints and hand-lettering enamels, so there's no need to invest a ton of money into a project like this. ■

Stenciling the Practice Fender

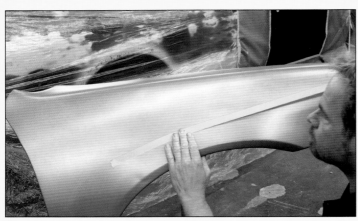

1 *Let the clear layers on each panel dry for several hours. Start laying out a basic location for the letters on the testing surface. I like masking tape for this because if you use a little tension on the end of the tape as you pull it you can make nice gradual curves, which is the way I want my letters to sit.*

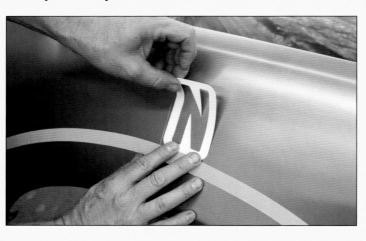

2 *Next, establish a center line for the sign using a ruler and a china marker. The china marker rubs off easily with mineral spirits or any mild solvent after you're finished lettering.*

3 *Beginning in the middle, use the tape as a guide to lay the letters out. Since the adhesive is low tac, it's easy to remove the stencil if you're not happy with the placement.*

Color Choices

Sign painting has always been considered a skilled craft that takes many years to master. The use of bold colors in ads was more and more popular as time progressed through the neon era of the 1920s through the 1960s. Color choice in signs and hand-painted advertisements was and still is very subjective, which gives us the option to choose colors based on our tastes, interior colors, and exterior colors of a particular build.

For your vintage signs, you can simply choose a color you think looks good or you can refer to a color wheel and find a compatible color. It always helps to either spray out or brush out the colors you want to use on a separate palate and compare it to the color of your project to check for compatibility. In our case, the practice panel will serve as our guide. There are hundreds of colors available from auto parts stores and home centers. Since our colors are green tones, we've stayed within that range of color for this project. Having said that, color choice is personal and subjective. You can use your imagination, go by examples from others, or just do what feels best to you and gives you the best effect.

4 Since it's a scrap fender, we thought it would be fun to name it appropriately. Doing a test panel like this liberating because there's no pressure if you make mistakes.

5 You have two options with stencils: you could use a wide lettering brush and fill in the stencils or use aerosol paint as we are doing. We're using aerosol paint because it is applied in very thin layers that are much easier to style. Because of that, we've got to mask around the stencil and protect the rest of the panel.

6 When you look closely at the edges of the letters, you can see that they're not fully contacting the surface. Leave this alone in order to create an effect.

7 Since the spray pattern from the can is small, you only need to mask 6 inches out from the panel.

Distressing Your Sign

Once you've stenciled on your colors and let them dry, carefully remove the stencils.

Now it is time to back-style or distress the sign. There are a number of ways to do this. Simply sanding the surface would give you an aged look. Many signs were very simple in nature with only a single color, so that may be a great choice. Personally, I like the use of drop shadows and highlights in graphics and sign it gives dimension to an otherwi flat panel. Those techniques are quit sophisticated in nature when don by a real sign painter, but if you' like me and respect the artform b

Our color is a weird muted brownish green, and it's a satin finish. Since it's a weak color (not bright), it's fairly transparent, which will give us the effect we're looking for with only a single coat.

As the paint dries, you can get a close look at the opacity even though it was a consistent coat. Since a lot of this color will be removed as we style the letters there's no need for a second coat.

A good habit to get into while unmasking is to pull the tape back away from itself rather than up away from the panel. This creates less tension on the panel and fewer tendencies to pull any paint up from under the tape.

Here's another example of proper tape removal techniqu Pull the tape backward against itself. If you're working on top of and trying to save original patina, you could pull weak paint right off of the metal.

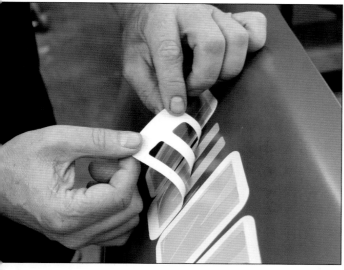

e letters come up easily but do require lifting one edge
ith a fingernail. This is a really good reason to make sure
ur protection coats are completely dry.

Since these stencils are reusable, we're saving them! The
backing plastic that came with them is the perfect way to
do this, and they're simply reapplied to their original position and placed back into the packaging.

The unmasked lettering looks old just
by virtue of the color. Simply sanding
through some of the letters would give
an authentic look, but we're taking
things a few steps further and giving
you some more practice techniques.

We'll be using 1-Shot enamel to create some detail and accents on the
letter surface. This paint is extremely
durable and relatively inexpensive.
This is a small sample of the 50-color
palate, as well as some high temperature reducer, which gives you the
ability to adjust how the paint flows.

don't possess the skill quite yet, I'll show you how to work around that shortcoming.

Early automobile manufacturers used expert pinstripers and sign painters to paint accents on body lines, which created attractive accents on vehicles prior to and during World War II. Sign painters were a very important part of the automotive industry, and the genre employed a lot of people in this very skilled and highly compensated trade. With the increasing addition of chrome-plated accents on vehicles, hand-applied striping was phased out of vehicle mass production, but it was still kept alive in the sign-painting trade.

Custom pinstriping has consistently been a part of the hot rodding culture and lifestyle since the early

Detailing the Letters on the Practice Fender

1 *We're going to be using a #00 squirrel hair striping brush as well as a #4 brush, which will give us a slightly thicker line. As this project progresses, you will quickly realize that I am a student of pinstriping and not a pinstriper. This is okay! The fact that I have limited skills in this art form should make you feel comfortable that you can get a similar result even if you've never picked up a brush.*

2 *First, we will use the color black to paint a drop shadow under the letters. This will appear to lift them off the panel. Use a #00 brush for this exercise.*

3 *After dipping the brush into the paint, use a palating technique to load paint all the way into the belly of the brush. This gives you the ability to paint long lines without frequent reloading.*

1950s when Kenneth Howard (aka Von Dutch) revolutionized striping as an art form with his bold style and fearless designs. His legacy lives on in the hands of many current artists who proudly draw influence from Von Dutch original designs.

Pinstriping brushes are typically made of squirrel hair, which is fibrous and holds paint well. Mac is the oldest manufacturer of striping brushes in the United States, creating brushes since 1891. There are many different brush sizes, each with its own pur-

pose, but an experienced painter typically has a favorite size that he can do multiple line sizes designs with. Some people quickly master striping techniques, others take longer to learn the skill, but nobody gets better without lots of practice!

4 Make several back and forth swipes through the paint on the magazine. Then practice dragging the brush and seeing how the lines look. I'm after smooth consistency with a tiny bit of resistance on the brush.

5 Before laying down stripes or shadows, we've got to remove the china marker. Do this by rubbing it off with a little mineral spirits on a rag. This mild solvent won't disturb the letters.

6 I was taught a trick by Rick Bacon, a talented custom painter and pinstriper from California who goes by "Arsonist" in his signed artwork. Use a yellow circle to remind you of where the sun is, which will tell you where shadows need to be. Knowing your light source will guide you to create a realistic effect.

Detailing the Letters on the Practice Fender CONTINUED

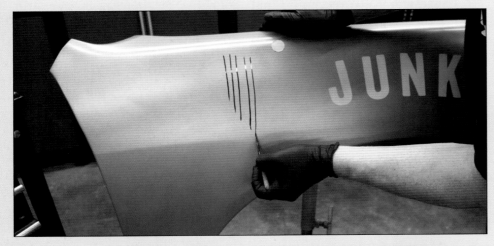

7 Since this is a practice panel, I'm going to practice a little on the fender, seeing what is a comfortable hand position and what is not. (Hint: this is not comfortable and not a good technique!)

8 With the sun to the left, the shadows belong on the right side of the letters. I'm placing my line just to the side of the actual letter wi some separation.

9 Here you can see the inconsistency of my lines. This will actually work in my favor when it comes to creating an aged effect. Wipe mistakes off with a shop towel and mineral spirits. The 1-Shot paint stays wet for a long time and allows you to remove it easily.

10 The next color we will use is polar white. Use the same palating technique as before, adding in reducer as necessary to get a consistent drag from the brush.

1 This time, practice on some black sheet metal. Test pressure and speed to control the line size.

12 Using the yellow circle as my guide again, the white will represent a spectral highlight or a reflection in the letter. This would happen on the side closest to the light source, so draw a line down to where the letter starts to curve. I'm placing a slight dot at the bottom of my highlights to add dimension.

13 Correcting mistakes at this stage is easy with mineral spirits and a towel. Smudges can be wiped up easily.

14 When you look at the sun icon, you can easily see the value in knowing the placement of your light source. The effect is simple and complete with a drop shadow and two-dimensional highlight.

Detailing the Letters on the Practice Fender CONTINUED

15 *After the 1-Shot paint has dried for a couple of hours, we can start styling for effect. We're using 1000-grit wet sandpaper to carefully remove paint a little at a time.*

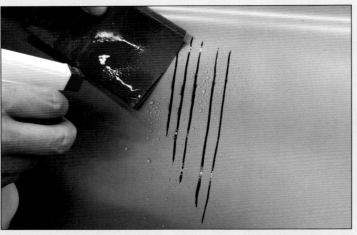

16 *Using water as a lubricant, saturate the surface of the panel as well as the sandpaper.*

17 *After just a few strokes of the sandpaper, the black color will wear through and reveal the texture of the clearcoat under the stripes.*

18 *When sanding the letters, focus the ball of your finger into the middle of the letter and remove as much of the spray paint as you feel needs to be gone so that it looks faded. Don't remove the shadows or highlights, but make them look faded too.*

19 After only a few minutes of sanding, the effect is complete! Quickly remove any residue so that it doesn't dry on the surface.

20 If you are satisfied with the effect, use a gray scuffing pad to even the sheen of the surrounding area.

21 Practicing several patina techniques on a single project will give you confidence and experience to move forward on your actual project.

1971 C10 Project

Practice is a confidence builder and will reward proper procedures at the same time as reveal bad techniques. There is a time investment for creating spray-out panels, practice panels, and sample boards, but most custom shops make a regular practice of doing a sample of the art to get the approval from the customer or test colors and designs. With a strategy for aging our shop truck signs, we can start the process of laying out the stencils and overall design on the 1971 C10 truck.

Letter stencils are not the only style available; there are custom airbrushing stencils that can be used to create amazing effects and designs. The Kustom Shop has a line of stencils that are used with an airbrush to create stripe patterns that look like pulled lines. We found this multi-layered design that will be a great centerpiece to our door sign. Even with bad techniques and limited skills, I could create an authentic design that looks period correct and naturally aged. These stencils will help create that illusion with a small investment in equipment and a few hours of your time.

Lettering the Door

1 For proper letter spacing, it always helps to establish a centerline on your panel. Use a china marker for a reference mark in the middle of the panel and at the top of the useable flat space on the door.

2 Add another reference on the bottom of the useable space and establish the center of the lower portion of the door.

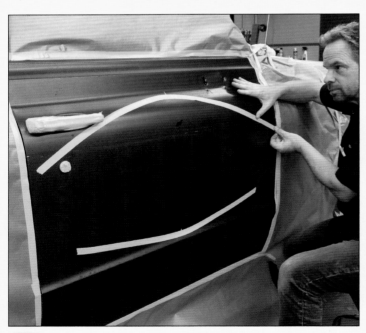

3 Use masking tape to give a gentle curve for the letter placement. I want the letters to surround a final design in the center.

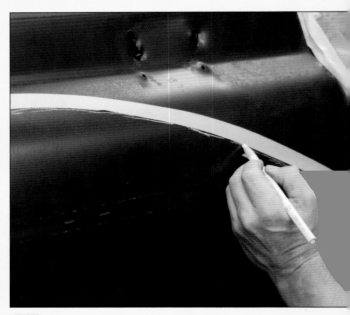

4 Remove the masking tape as soon as possible so the glue doesn't leave an impression on the clearcoat or lift any paint off the panel. The china marker will serve as your guide after you remove the masking tape.

5 Use the block letters on the bottom to spell the word garage. This process may take several tries, but the low-tac adhesive on the back of the stickers is very forgiving and allows for removal as many times as necessary.

6 The script-styled stencils are roughly 2 inches wide, so mark spacing or 2.5 inches to allow for the curve in the layout.

7 There needs to be separation between the two words for legibility. Take some time to get the spacing right.

8 Because you will be spraying paint on the stencils, the edges need to be masked to keep overspray off the rest of the panel.

9 Rather than fill in the space with tape, use masking paper. Avoid contact as much as possible with the rest of the door panel.

Lettering the Door CONTINUED

10 Apply a single medium coat to all of the letters. If you wanted a different color on the different letter styles, now is the time to make that decision.

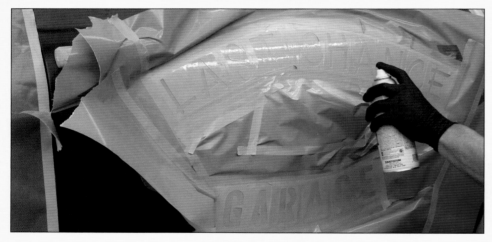

11 You can see clearly the inconsistency of a single coat of this color. That is the effect we want; it will help minimize edge buildup on the stencils.

12 After the paint dries for about an hour, unmask the stencil. Use the technique of folding the tape against itself to remove it.

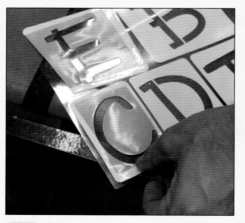

13 Place the letters back on their backing cards to save them for another use later.

14 Here you can see where the stencil has lifted. This is a mistake that will work in our favor! Don't freak out if things like this happen; there is always a way to fix a mistake. Besides, it just may create an interesting effect.

Stenciling the Design

1 *Another set of stencils will give us our design in between the slogan. We are using Kafka-designed stencils that can be stacked together and sprayed through to give a pinstripe effect while using an airbrush. We'll use our spray paint instead.*

2 *Here you can see the intricate detail of the stencils. With this, you can incorporate multiple colors, one layer at a time.*

3 *When you are happy with the placement in the center of the panel, carefully mark the edges of the stencil to get the exact same placement of the next layer.*

4 *Mask off the area around the outside of the stencil with 6-inch paper to control overspray.*

Stenciling the Design CONTINUED

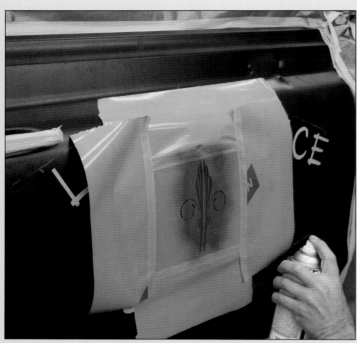

5 Spray a light-but-even coat of your first color through the detail of the stencil.

6 Peel the stencil slowly back, being careful not to allow contact with any of the panel.

7 You can use a heat gun to force dry the thin layer of paint between steps. Wait about 15 to 20 minutes before applying the next stencil and color.

8 Place the next design in the exact same position as the first stencil, using the alignment marks you created in step 3.

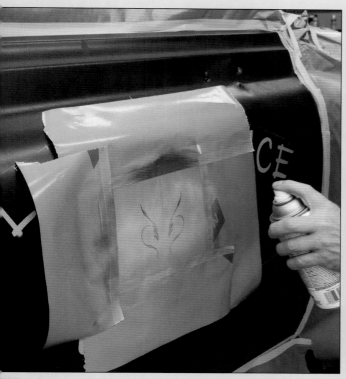

9 Apply your second color. This should be applied as a medium-wet coat as well.

10 It's exciting to reveal the layers of the design! Carefully peeling the stencil is critical so you don't smudge the colors.

11 Place the last stencil in the exact same position in order for the design to interweave as intended.

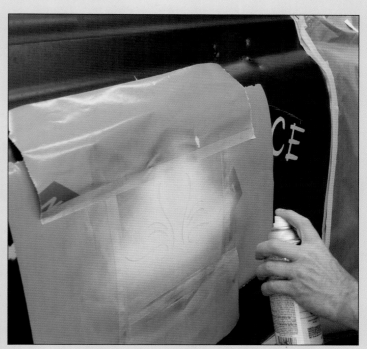

12 Add the third color. Our final color was a turquoise that has a 1950s feel to it, which adds to the era we're trying to recreate.

Stenciling the Design CONTINUED

13 *The completed design plays perfectly with the original patina or the door.*

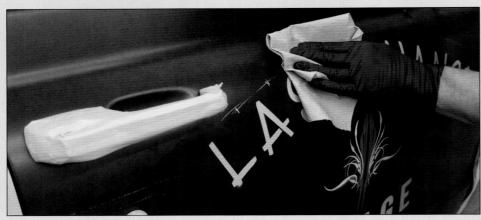

14 *Use mineral spirits and a soft towel to remove the china marker reference lines from the artwork.*

Adding Drop Shadow and Highlights

1 *Use the techniques you practiced on our first panel here. Place the location of the sun to the right side of the panel.*

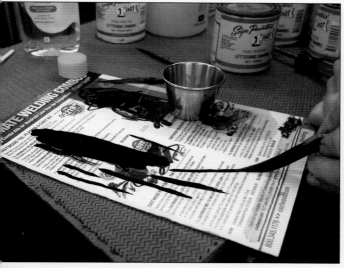

2 Use the #4 striping brush for a wider drop shadow. Follow the steps of palating and loading the brush, dding reducer as necessary.

3 Apply the drop shadows. You can see that my technique is not much better, but my confidence is up! The drop shadows are roughly 1/4-inch wide and fall on the left side of the letters this time. I removed the gloves, which were giving me too much traction as I pulled the brush across the panel. Just be careful to avoid skin contact with the paint.

4 Use mineral spirits to recover from mistakes, but keep in mind that mistakes can enhance the effect of patinizing. Not all mistakes need to be removed.

5 Due to the design difference of the scripted letters on top, the drop shadows are a little more challenging. Remember to step back and take a look at your sun marker from time to time as a guide.

Adding Drop Shadow and Highlights *CONTINUED*

6 With the drop shadows complete, let the paint dry for abo 15 minutes so we don't smudge it wi our next color.

7 Move on to the second color. We're getting creative and making our own, starting with purple I'm using a pipette to dip into the paint can without making a mess.

8 Adding a small amount of purple to the polar white color created an interesting lavender that will serve as our spectral highlight. Choose your highlight color now.

9 For this step, use the #00 fine brush. It leaves a ve fine line that's easy to control.

0 *You can choose to change colors for highlights and drop shadows. We're switching to Primrose Yellow for the highlights on the bottom block letters. Make sure to thoroughly clean your brushes with thinner, reducer, or acetone before changing colors.*

11 *The yellow highlights pop off of the letters immediately as well as complement the green panel. Notice how I'm bracing my hand with my other hand against the panel. With some practice, you'll get comfortable with bracing.*

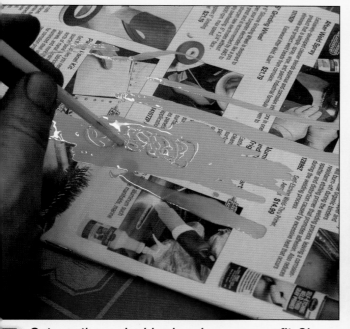

2 *Get creative and add color where you see fit. Since we've got some yellow on the palate, we added some detail accents on the design using the wrong end of paint brush.*

13 *This model painting brush from a hobby shop has a nicely rounded end that holds enough paint for a single dot for an accent. Have fun creating a unique design.*

Finishing Touches

1 *Wait a few hours for the paint to dry. Then, use 400-grit sandpaper to remove material from the letters and start distressing the detail areas. Focus the pad of your finger on the center of the letters and be careful not to sand off all of the highlights or shadows. This is the same technique used on the practice panel.*

2 *With the styling on the letters and design complete, run a scuffing pad over the surface again to make sure the next layer of clearcoat will properly adhere.*

3 *If you left the panel alone at this stage, it would still look good. But, you can clearly see the sanding marks from the distressing techniques.*

4 *Sealing the work with another coat of matte clearcoat brings back the consistency of the whole panel and protects the work from further deterioration.*

5 *Because you applied two coats of clear under the art, there is a protective film over the original patina. When the area around the letters was sanded, the original paint was protected and wasn't disturbed. The final layer of clear buries the sanding scratches in the ground coat of clear, and makes them invisible. You can clearly see that the consistent matte sheen has been restored to the panel, and the sanding marks are now hidden.*

6 Mission accomplished! Our patina matches the original aged look of the truck, and it's a natural and authentic style of sign that looks as if it has been sitting in the sun for decades.

7 Keeping your striping brushes clean and prepped for the next use is very important! Striping brushes develop a personality over the years, and the more you use em, the more you get familiar with their characteristics. e heard of people using kerosene, engine oil, and ineral spirits as well, but Rick Harris advised me to use aby oil, and that's my advice to you. Baby oil keeps the airs supple and primed while you're not using them.

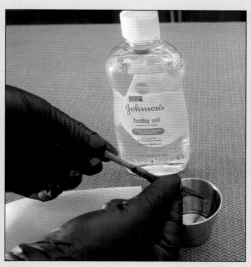

8 Dip your brush into the baby oil then squeeze the excess out from the brush. It's now safe to put them back into storage.

Summary

It seems counterintuitive that ou can take advantage of a lack skill when it comes to custom inting; however, that's exactly hat you can use to your advantage patina painting projects. The consistent striping lines, once ey're sanded through a little, look e aged pinstriping even more. sing stencils gives the illusion of professional job that was done many years ago, and removing layers off the top gives a natural faded look. Single-stage noncatalyzed paints, such as Dupli-Color's Paint Shop system, work hand-in-hand with their line of rattle cans, so you have compatibility between colors, layers, and a protective clearcoat overtop of your art if you choose to do so.

The only real rules that you need to follow are the rules of solvent and the rules of adhesion, which are simple and fundamental across the board in any painting scenario. You must allow solvent to evacuate before moving on to the next step, and you must have either mechanical or chemical adhesion between your layers of paint. These are easy concepts to learn and understand. Using these two simple rules will allow your art and creativity to come through and give your own personal touch to any patina project.

A COMPLETE PATINA PAINT JOB

If you've never done it before, attempting any style of all-over paint job can be intimidating. It's a big job that takes a lot of space and a lot of time, but the rewards are definitely worth the effort. In my career as a professional painter, I've shot hundreds if not thousands of paint jobs over the past 30 years, but I realize that it's a daunting process if it's your first time.

The fauxtina paint job we're going to show you is very different from a conventional paint job that has the goal of emulating a *new* factory finish. When you're undertaking a big project, there's always a certain amount of stress involved with trying to achieve your goals, especially when that goal is a perfect conventional paint job. With a factory finish or a high-end restoration or custom paint job, you're worried about using the most meticulous prep procedures and near-perfect technique. There are so many things that you have to do correctly and perfectly to achieve a perfect paint job that it is intimidating, even to a seasoned pro.

With this paint job, our goal is to create the illusion of decades of wear, and in some cases even damage to the paint and sheet metal. The whole strategy is changed, and a new

The Volkswagen Beetle is a fun car, so we wanted a fun paint job that was viv[...] but aged and told the story of a long life of colorful adventures. After paint, th[...] car will be fit with a new interior and a souped-up flat-four VW engine that wil[...] make it a fast, reliable, and attractive car, complete with custom paint. This w[...] be a show car that the owner is not afraid to drive!

Paint Strategies

In a restoration or collision repair respray, your ground coats and undercoats must be applied for very specific reasons and fully within the rules of the products. They're forever protected by the topcoats, whether that is a base clear or single-stage system. In the case of our fauxtina job, we're going to use a very different paint strategy, working from the ground coat up with the intention of exposing the layers of undercoats using sanding and abrasive techniques. In effect, we're building up our paint job upside-down and reverse engineering the aging process so that we can style and patinize to our liking.

In this chapter, we're going to show you how to create a full vehicle patina paint job using many of the techniques that we've practiced in the pages of this book. We'll create an authentic-looking faded and worn-out paint job on a 1974 Volkswagen Beetle that is based on our artist rendering. We'll use photos of many different stages and styles of patina as inspiration for different effects on this car. This can be considered a full-size final exam of sorts, since we'll have the opportunity to try out all sorts of different effects on a vehicle that is as close to a timeless design as we have seen over the past few decades. The shape of the car lends itself to patina.

et of rules is in place. This is where gets fun! The freedom that one has eating a patina paint job is actually liberating and exciting! Knowing at you can relax just a little from e rigid cleanliness that's necessary a collision repair booth or on a estoration-quality paint job feels od and takes some pressure off.

is 1950 Chevrolet truck was a very popular build on the television show RUCKS! We used a photo from the internet of an Arizona truck that had sat the sun deteriorating for 50 years to inspire the styling of this vehicle. Other otable features are the use of raw copper where there normally would be rome-plated bumpers and grille, adding to the character of this truck.

is 1965 Mustang Fastback was the project of a show on DIY Network, where e restored portions of the car back to life. Film industry prop-styling tech-ques, such as dulling sprays, matte-finish clearcoats, talcum powder, and ist embedded in a water soluble spray were used to create the appearance f neglected storage. Older parts were changed out to facilitate projects for the eries. (Photo Courtesy Melissa Cross)

This is an original Mustang interior showing decades of wear, or is it? Parts can be easily switched and changed to give the look of a worn-out vehicle. (Photo Courtesy Melissa Cross)

The restored Mustang is beautiful! Television magic was applied and this is actually the Mustang that we started with in the same restored condition. Through the use of patina painting, prop-styling techniques, and standard restoration techniques, the combination of back-styling and automotive restoration gave us the ability to show an amazing transformation on this vehicle, install performance upgrades on the body and chassis, and work within a time frame that suited the production goals of the TV series. There was no deception in this episodic series; the projects and upgrades were real, the process was faithful to an actual restoration, and the tutorials for the upgrades and projects were carried over from standard restoration procedures. This car was a magnificent example, both before and after the episodes were finished. (Photo Courtesy Melissa Cross)

Ian Johnson of Big Tire Garage has a reputation for building world-class off-road vehicles on television and in magazines. Shop Truck is a hybrid of sorts, using a Jeep YJ front end, aluminum body tub, and aftermarket chassis loaded with top-of-the-line off-road components. We transformed this vehicle several years ago with my patina techniques along with some cool touches, including raw copper, rust from uncoated metal, and modern commercial signs via stickers on the doors, which look authentic even up close. Notice the use of copper-plated bumpers and genuine rust mixed in with recently patinized paint. Ian Johnson's Shop Truck is a very strong off-road vehicle that draws a crowd at every event with its cool appearance and awesome performance.

is 1974 Volkswagen Beetle has been modified and orked on extensively over the years. It has made its ay through several sets of hands and finally back to its rrent owner, who chose it as his first car. It sports a ediocre single-stage paint job that is covering up several odifications, including shaved turn signal lights on the ont fenders, a shaved (removed) hood handle, and cus-m fiberglass rear fenders that will accommodate a much der wheel and tire combination. Overall, the condition this bug is fair, and the paint job is holding up alright nsidering the years of neglect.

The body is in relatively good condition with minimal rust. The color is uninspiring to say the least, so we'll be choosing a much better-looking retro color combination to create the cool paint job we want to see. The rear fenders have a custom lighting design that features recessed tail-lights that have a retro blue-dot lens. This will play to our favor, and will also give us another way to back-style the appearance of this car. Overall, this car is in decent condition and will serve our purpose of providing a platform to demonstrate patina painting techniques.

The reason I wrote this book in e first place was because I have d so much fun creating an over-l patina look on several projects ve had my hands on. I've done tina jobs on vehicles for televi-n shows and for off-road buggies d crawlers, and have thoroughly joyed the freedom, creativity, and pression that this format gives e as an artist. Using my imagi-tion and knowing that there is wrong outcome is incredibly npowering and quite honestly n. Having said that, we are always ided by the goal of creating real-ic, authentic-looking patina, and high-quality paint job.

Tools and Equipment

There are a lot of tools to con-der, as well as important details, ch as good ventilation, proper fety equipment, good lighting,

and protecting your tools and other equipment that you don't want overspray to settle on. Masking is another important procedure, and we'll show you how to mask off your car so that overspray doesn't accumulate on the glass, seals, and trim.

Unlike a restoration-quality paint job, a full-patina paint job doesn't require the same controlled environment to paint in. Flaws can become signatures, mistakes become character markings, and it can all contribute to an overall realistic patina. You will need a safe working environment, good safety equipment, and some basic

Shop prep starts with making sure we have airflow and a safe environment to spray paint in. Not everyone has a spray booth, but you can still get great results without one. Inexpensive furnace filters taped to the door and floor will filter air and keep out bugs and debris while we paint.

spray equipment, but you don't necessarily need a spray booth. We sprayed in our shop and used the roll-up doors to create airflow that would clear overspray effectively. Using inexpensive furnace filters taped across the partially opened garage door, we made sure we had reasonably clean air flowing through our shop.

On the other end of our shop, we used the same size filters taped to the floor and the bottom of the door to create a crossflow of air that would evacuate any overspray that might otherwise build up and be dangerous. We used efficient HVLP spray

The opposite end of the shop gets another row of filters as well. This creates a crossflow of air and will help clear the air of overspray as we spray paint.

Any time you're using pneumatic tools, you must make sure you've go adequate air to run them. For what little spraying we're going to be doin on this small car, you could get by with a much smaller compressor tha our 7-hp 120-gallon unit, which has more than enough clean dry air deliv ery capacity for any painting project.

guns set to relatively low air pressure and applyed our layers carefully, since this is not at all like a conventional paint job.

You will need an air compressor capable of delivering air for at least three minutes at a time without starting up. This keeps your air cool and gives you consistent air delivery. There are specific rules for conventional paint delivery, such as having at least a 5-hp pump with 60 gallons of storage for an allover paint job. You can get away with much less air volume doing patina, as there are multiple alternate application techniques that don't use air delivery at all. Our compressor is a 7.5-hp dual-stage compressor with a 120-gallon air storage tank. Although it's more than 20 years old, there's still plenty of life left in it as long as service is done regularly.

You'll need enough paper to properly sand the entire vehicle. Typically, it takes me a 4 x 6 piece of sandpaper per panel. Multiply that times roughly 10 panels per vehicle, tells you that you'll probably need a dozen or so sheets of paper. Although major suppliers provide sleeves of paper containing 50 pieces, companies geared toward hobby painters and DIY jobs offer smaller quantities for much less money. If you plan on doing more than one paint job, it may make more sense to buy a sleeve of paper, but if it's going to sit in a drawer or on a shelf you may want to spend a little more per sheet and buy less overall quantity.

Surface Preparation

Surface prep is not much different with fauxtina paint than any other paint. You *must* have good adhesion, and you *must* use good preparation techniques. One of my rules is "the harder it is to reach, t more important it is to reach i Using scuffing pads in tight corne and using the proper grit sandp per are very important. Having sa that, you can get away with slight coarser grits of paper when maki fauxtina, simply because some the flaws that happen with coar grit sanding marks coming throug the top layers add character and m actually look (worse) better.

Automotive Sanding

1 *For basic prep, we're using a dual-action sander, 320-grit sandpaper, and an interface pad so that the sander and paper conform to the rounded shape of this car body.*

2 *The 320-grit sandpaper has more than enough grit to sufficiently rough the surface up for new paint. The pads attach to the sander with a hook and loop system, which makes them easy to attach and remove during use.*

3 *The interface pad also attaches with a hook and loop system. With its 3/8-inch thickness, it will conform to many different surface shapes and still maintain contact of the paper to the painted surface.*

4 *You can clearly see the benefit of the foam interface pad here. The squish of the pad will allow us to quickly prep the rounded panels without making flat spots and digging holes in the painted surface.*

5 *Sand the flat surfaces of the body using a slow speed and medium pressure. This allows efficient movement to prep the paint while also inspecting the surface for flakes, cracks, and other anomalies.*

6 *The sander won't reach every part of the paint, and turning the pad on its side to get into tighter spots is a serious no-no! Hand sanding is definitely necessary in these spots.*

Removing accessories, trim, and lighting parts will depend on the extent of your work and the plan you have for creating patina. One would typically remove every piece of trim and glass to do a proper paint job, but a patina job may require overspray on some parts to create character. We've decided at this point to remove wipers, handles, and what little trim is left on this car.

Reassembly is made much easier if parts are labeled as they are removed!

Our 1939 Ford taillights, complete with blue-dots, are very cool, and will definitely stay! There's opportunity to easily age the lenses and chrome while they are off the car and still keep them legal and safe.

The outer door handles were painted body color at some time in the 1990s, when that was the fad. This is where you have the choice to try to reuse what's there or find vintage handles that suit your design. We've got a plan for these!

Tear down or not to tear down? You need to ask yourself the question of whether or not you want to remove mirrors, door handles, trim parts, and lights in order to do your paint job. If you look at a wonderfully bad paint job that is 30 years old, chances are you're going to see paint that is bridged up over the gaps and gaskets between your door handles and sheet metal or window moldings.

If this is what you're trying to recreate, you probably want to leave all the accessories in place while you paint and even do a poor job masking to allow bridging and overspray. If you're trying to recreate an original barn-find-style paint job that has never been repaired and has only its original paint coat on, then you'll want to remove all the trim, handles, mirrors, and accessories so that you *don't* end up with telltale signs of a respray. Each has its own charm, and more importantly, each has its own painting strategy. You need to have formed a plan before you get to the point of actually painting.

With either strategy, you'll need to set aside enough time to properly prep the vehicle. And that means that you need to account for at least one hour per panel for proper prep, and then have a strategy for applying the paint itself. If you're a weekend warrior like most of us, you may want to dedicate one weekend for prep; the following weekend for paint application; a third session for sanding, airbrush signage, or detailing; and perhaps an overall sealing-in session of your artwork.

Large surface areas are not difficult to work with, but strategy is required with revealing and styling your fauxtina. Applying the layers in the proper order and reverse engineering your job is key to a predictable result. At this stage, you should have completed multiple practice exercises, practice panels, and you should know the recipe to achieving your goal.

There are only two types of adhesion when it comes to paint coating: mechanical adhesion and chemical adhesion. Mechanical adhesion sanding scratches and tooth in the surface to provide something for the paint to physically lock in and bond to. Chemical adhesion is where one coating crosslinks with another and the two become chemically bonded together. The first is achieved by mechanical sanding, the second by chemistry, and there is *nothing* in between, so you must properly prep your surfaces for paint adhesion either way.

The rules are different with patina, but there are definitely still rules. You want your work to last many years and still have the look of a quality job. Don't make the mistake that a lot of people make and think that because you're creating a look that resembles decay and disrepair that fundamental techniques don't apply.

Preparing the Surface

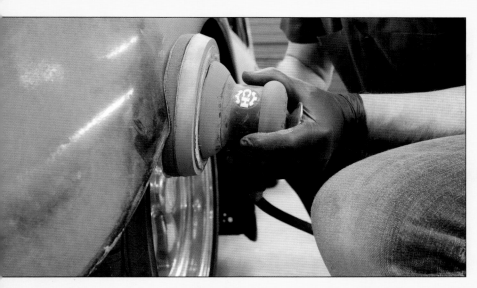

1 *The power of the interface pad is demonstrated here. Even though our paint prep is not conventional, it must be thorough! There's no excuse for unsanded areas, and the new paint job simply won't stick to unsanded paint.*

2 *We'll keep these chips intact and restore the glorious crusty look of them with our new paint job. Using the sanding pad on these areas would smooth them over and "fix" them, which is not what we want.*

3 *Use the dual-action sander on the flat panels. When we were finished with the dual-action sander, we had used a total of eight pads for most of the surface area on the car.*

4 *Follow up on the sander step with red scuffing pads. These are made from random strands of fiber that have grit particles glued to the strands. This gives you the ability to place scratches into a surface in areas that are impossible to get to with a sander. It also gives you the ability to sand a surface properly without changing the shape of it or smoothing over details (such as our rock chips).*

Preparing the Surface CONTINUED

5 *The scuffing pad gets folded, pressed, and pushed into the recesses and style lines of the car body until all of the shiny spots of unsanded paint are gone. This is a seemingly thankless job in the moment but a totally necessary and important prep task.*

6 *The scuffing pads allow us to properly abrade all of the crevasses in this body detail.*

7 *We'll use only a single red pad on the entire project. Supplies are expensive, but if you use them well, they save you time.*

8 *Use a dust filter mask while scuffing the car, since we're doing this dry. Wet sanding takes away the dust and eliminates the need for the mask, but it is messy to work around.*

The surface *must* be clear of dust and debris before applying the new paint. Most shops would roll the vehicle outside and blow it down with compressed air, removing any debris on the surface. Ours didn't run and wouldn't roll very well, so we used a vacuum to pull the dust off the panel and followed that with a two-stage cleaning procedure. First we used a solvent cleaner, and then we followed it with a foaming glass cleaner to remove any other contaminants that the solvent didn't remove.

After cleaning, conventional masking techniques are used to cover any areas that you don't want overspray or paint coatings to cover. Masking is straightforward and much easier to do with a bodyshop masking cart that applies the tape to the paper as you remove it from the roll. This is a luxury, but if you're doing a lot of masking, it's a big time saver.

Cleaning and Masking

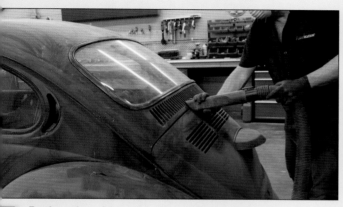

Rather than blow the dust off the surface with an air hose, use a wet/dry vacuum to pull the dust off of and out of the vehicle panels and gaps. This is a much cleaner prep step than a blower, and it ultimately gets the surface cleaner. You can see the rear window gasket standing out away from the body, ready for paint.

2 The next steps involve a wax and grease removal wipe followed by a glass cleaner. A two-step cleaning process will get rid of solvent-based and organic cleaners, giving you a very clean surface to spray on. If you don't have access to autobody supplies, you can use naphtha for your solvent wipe down. Our pump sprayer does a nice job of atomizing the cleaner without too much mess.

Gloves are a must at this stage! Not only to control the mess, but to keep from your skin absorbing chemicals. We're using paper shop towels to evacuate the cleaner and dust as it is suspended in the cleaner.

4 After the solvent wipe down, go back over all of the panels with the aerosol glass cleaner for a final cleaning step before paint. Even if your goal is creating a messy rat rod look, there are rules to go by in the paint shop, and a clean surface is high on the list.

Cleaning and Masking CONTINUED

5 *We couldn't get our rope under the rear side glass because the rubber was old and tight, so we're going to mask and paint up to the rubber. Tape will not stick to oxidized or dirty rubber gaskets, so use solvent cleaner to prep the rubber for masking.*

6 *We're outlining everything that will be masked off with 3/4-inch masking tape. On the raised glass gaskets, we wrapped the tape under the exposed lip.*

7 *Under the engine cover, tape off the seal and cover the transmission housing to protect it from over-spray. This engine will be air cooled, and there are many louvers that allow airflow that will also allow overspray into the engine compartment. If you don't want paint on it, cover it up!*

8 *Although not totally necessary, a masking cart like this is a wonderful tool to have! This style costs less than $100 and has options for multiple size paper rolls and storage for tape and cutting tools.*

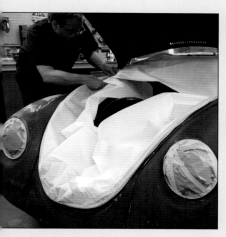

9 *Mask anything that you don't want overspray to get into. Masking also prevents paint from blowing out from under panels and into the wet paint.*

10 *Single-edge razor blades are a staple in my paint shop. Care must be used not to cut too far into the paint or you could promote chipping. Taping the door handle holes from the outside is another way to prevent blowback of debris from holes in the bodywork.*

1 Mask doorjambs with 6-inch masking paper to protect the interior from overspray as well.

12 *Covering the shop floor prevents paint from creating a permanent silhouette of the car on the concrete. This masking paper was purchased from a home center and taped in place with 1½-inch masking tape. You can see the clear plastic on the wheels. Another option would be to remove the wheels completely.*

13 *To protect our clothing, we're using a disposable spray suit. These cost less than $10 each and will save your clothes from overspray.*

14 *Drop cloths are inexpensive to buy and will do a great job of protecting tools, benches, and equipment from paint overspray as well. The plastic will also help keep debris from blowing up off of counters and from behind benches into wet paint.*

We've decided to leave the windows in place since the seals are relatively new and the car didn't leak. We'll show you a technique using 1/4-inch nylon rope that gives the appearance that you've removed the glass for the paint job.

The rope is slipped between the bottom of the seal and the car body, lifting the seal off the panel.

You can see clearly here how the rope allows paint to blow in under the window seals during the paint job. When the rope is removed, the seal falls on top of the new paint, giving the illusion that the glass was removed. This also ensures that the paint won't build up outside and against the window rubber, creating a weak and brittle edge

Spray Techniques

Practice makes perfect. And practice gives you control over your spray gun. Even with a patina paint job, one still needs to have control over their equipment and understand how to properly use a paint gun in order to get an even coating of paint on a panel or vehicle. There are specific rules of spraying that need to be followed, beginning with consistency. I have developed a dry-training system called the "Spray Coach" that is available from Paintucation.com, and it teaches the muscle memory of perfect paint application before you actually commit to your spray job.

You need to have a clear understanding of what good technique feels like, and the only way to do that is to practice! I recommend practicing with water-based craft paint on cardboard then graduate to the actual paint system that you're going to be using for your paint job. In our case, we'll use the Dupli-Color Paint Shop system that is available in multiple retail outlets and online.

We've determined that the rubber gaskets on the front and rear glass are supple enough to leave in place and work with without having to remove them for proper paint application. Using a body shop technique, we'll lift up the edge of the seal just enough for paint to blow under the seal. When the rope is removed, the seal falls back on top of the panel and gives a tidy appearance with no paint buildup on the edge of the gasket.

When pouring paint into a spray gun, I *always* recommend pouring through a paint strainer, except today. A little debris or trash blown into our paint job will add character to the ground coat, and as I expose my layers, the debris will be exposed as well and lend an authentic look as I style my paint. Rules apply, but some are broken with patina painting!

Painting for patina is different from painting to resemble a factory paint job. You need to think about things from the bottom to the top. We're using a three-layer strategy for this project. The first layer is the black ground coat over all of the body panels. Spraying this first color will happen the same way a single coat of conventional paint job happens. Use a 50-percent overlap on each pass and make smooth transitions from one section to another until you've painted a smooth, wet, and even coat on the entire outer surface of the car

Safe Shop Practices

Safe shop practices are a must with any paint job! The Dupli-Color system does not require a hardener, making it much safer to use, but that doesn't mean you can compromise on safety. It just means that you can approach safety a little differently. You still need to wear gloves to keep from absorbing solvents and chemicals into your skin, and you still need to protect your respiratory system with a good-quality mask that fits correctly. I recommend using a spray suit to protect your clothing as well. Paint stinks and if it gets into your clothing, your clothing stinks! Not to mention the fact that a spray suit will protect your paint job from lint, hair, and other debris from falling into your paint job. The suit we're using cost less than $10 and can be tossed away after use. ∎

We are using the Dupli-Color Paint Shop system. Paint Shop is available in most automotive retail stores and requires no catalyst or reducer, meaning it's ready to spray right out of the can. This is a user-friendly paint that requires basic safety equipment and common sense to spray it.

Dupli-Color has several accessories that go with its paint system. Strainers, lacquer thinner for cleanup, and aerosol primers for detail work are all available. The other products we'll be using are the matte clearcoat, which we'll use as a finish coat to protect all our patina artwork once we're finished (as we did after painting the aged signs on the truck door).

The Eastwood Concours spray gun we're using is an HVLP gun that requires very little air volume to spray. We have a 1.3 fluid tip installed, which is perfect for the very thin viscosity of the Dupli-Color paint. The combination of both means that we'll be able to spray with relatively low air pressure (20 psi) and get great coverage with minimal overspray.

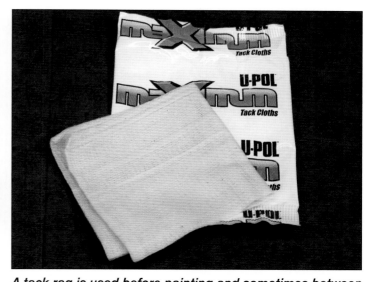

A tack rag is used before painting and sometimes between coats if debris falls onto the surface. Tack rags work best if taken out of the package and unfolded a few minutes before use.

Safety glasses, gloves, and a good charcoal respirator mask are a necessity! Just because there isn't a catalyst with this paint system doesn't mean you can cheat on safety. Overspray mist is very dangerous and toxic and needs to be treated with respect.

Spraying the Ground Coat

1 *The black ground coat is premixed and ready to spray right out of the can (once you've stirred thoroughly). This will simulate the original primer that Volkswagen may have applied on the bare steel body at the assembly plant. (At least that's our story!)*

2 *Normally, I will insist that you strain your paint into the spray gun cup, but not this time. If there are tin anomalies or paint particles that are stirred up and sprayed onto our ground coat, it will only give us characte as we expose the layers of our paint story by sanding.*

3 *Tack the surface of the car once before spraying. Inspect our surface one last time to make sure everything is sanded properly.*

4 *Make slow and controlled passes with the gun about 6 inches off of the panel, overlapping 50 percent at each pass 50. This creates a smooth layer of paint that is even on all panels.*

It's very important to be comfortable while spraying so you have complete control of the equipment. nding your comfort zone and working where you can sily reach is important! Once you've found the extent of ur reach, move to the next area. We're starting our black at on the top, and then moving from the rear to the front the car. First one quarter panel, then the other, then the ar, then on to the doors, then the front fenders and hood.

6 The bodywork on this car is like a geometric experiment, but don't get trapped into trying to follow every style line and curve. Treat your vehicle like a big box, keep your gun 6 inches off the panel, and keep a steady pace as your overlap by 50 percent, and you'll end up with an even coat.

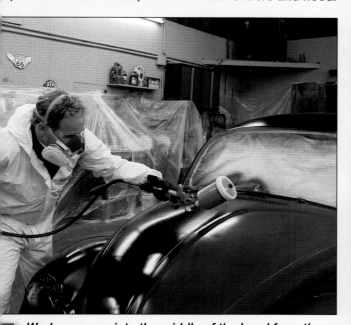

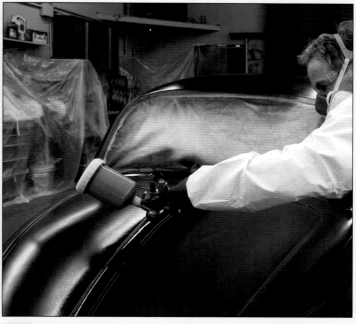

Work your way into the middle of the hood from the passenger fender. Once you reach the middle, step ound to the side, find the wet edge in the middle, and work the other side from there. This keeps every overlapped ss one on top of the other, much like a layer of shingles.

8 This paint dries quickly, but it's important not to hurry. Once your coat is completely finished and the car is covered in black, let it dry for 20 minutes. Clean the spray gun and move to the next layer.

Spraying the Primer Layer

1 We're using red oxide for our primer layer on top of the black ground coat, which will give us a nice color to expose when we style our paint job. Dupli-Color doesn't make a red oxide primer at this time in the Paint Shop system, so we're making our own using a blend that we created from the existing color palate. Chapter 5 on color will guide you if you want to do this step as well, but you will need to do some experimenting and spray samples to make sure your color is what you want. We're mixing a full quart starting with 500 grams of Hugger Orange.

2 To darken the orange and make it dirty, we added 100 grams of Jet Black.

3 Next, 150 grams of Performance Red gave us the oxide color and made our color identical to a 1960s red oxide color that will offset our turquoise nicely.

4 The result is a beautifully horrible red oxide that will become our second layer.

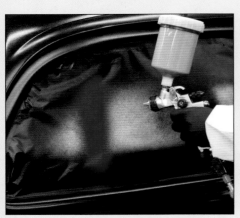

5 Always test your spray pattern on something other than your project! The masked window works well, and our pattern looks perfect.

6 Apply your second coat. Be sure to follow the strategy you created during your test design. For example, we did not paint an even coat of the primer. Instead, we only applied the red oxide to places that we know will be exposed from styling and sanding. There's no need to coat the entire vehicle with this color. You need to have a good idea where you're going to be showing wear on the panels, and we're following our rendering closely. If you don't have a rendering or photo to follow, just remember where the sun is and how paint wears out and ages: from the top down.

7 Create wear areas based on your rendering. Ours is placed on the driver's door opening where a lot of contact would be made by an arm or even excessive UV damage.

8 You can see the strategy of the red oxide here. The top gets the most sun and will have the most degraded look, but the tops of the rounded panels will be exposed as well.

9 Spray all areas that need the primer layer. Spraying the air intake vents red gives us the option of detailing them later.

10 Once you are satisfied with the placement of the red oxide primer, let it sit for at least 30 minutes to dry. This way masking tape and contact won't mar the paint or peel it off the panels.

Spraying the White Insert

1 Our vehicle has a white insert between the fenders (see rendering in chapter 4 on page 44). We masked the front and rear fenders as well as the hood to avoid a buildup of overspray that will interfere with our styling later on.

2 Our washed-out white formula calls for a small amount of yellow (800:1 ratio) to give it an off-white look. So we'll mix up enough to spray the sides. Dupli-Color Paint Shop colors cover well, so we won't need more than a full quart.

3 Testing our pattern on the masked window showed us that we're ready to spray. Remember to clean your spray gun between color changes so you don't contaminate each new color.

4 Here you can clearly see the 50-percent overlap of my spray pattern. You can also see that the color not fully covering the dark undercoat. You seldom get complete coverage in a single coat of any paint, so have patience and be ready to apply at least two coats to get full saturation.

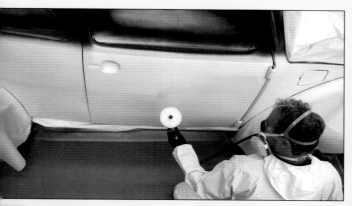

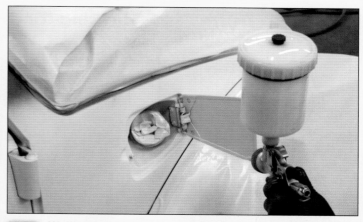

5 The second coat of white covers nicely and will be all we need on these side panels. Take a look at the top of the door frame. Notice the overspray that happens since I did not tape off the side panels at the top. This is not a mistake, and it will help us in styling later on.

6 We'll paint inside the fuel door as well, which will create authentic detail when someone fills this car with fuel later on. It also gives us a nice light color to create fuel stains on!

7 Two coats will get us the coverage that we need without applying so much paint that it's difficult to expose layers with sanding.

8 After 30 minutes of dry time (which is almost exactly how long it takes to clean a spray gun properly), we can remove our masking paper.

Masking for the Final Topcoat

1 *Cover up the white panels to spray our final topcoat. Using the tape as a knife edge and sliding it into the space between the sides and fenders will help get crisp masking lines.*

2 *If needed, carefully mask the top style line and dividing line for two colors. Using a long piece of tape pulled tightly helps us create a very straight and controlled line, just like a factory two-tone.*

3 *Use a razor blade (a staple in my shop because they come in handy for many reasons, one of which is detailed masking techniques) to c the tape. This gives you a crisp line where you need it.*

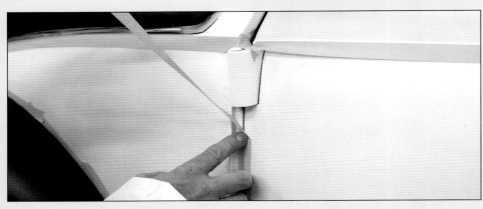

4 *Tape the door gaps from the outside to prevent blow-through from the back side of the panel and to control overspray.*

5 *Once the sides are outlined with 3/4-inch masking tape, f in the center with masking paper. Th is called a positive mask on the side*

6 It's important to completely cover the white panels before the next color. This creates a clean job and eliminates work from having to clean up blow-through and overspray drift under the paper.

7 Use tack paper on the panels once more before spraying the final color.

Spraying the Final Topcoat

1 The formula for our Tarnished Turquoise color is easy to follow, if you want to recreate it. It closely resembles several colors used widely in the 1950s and will look perfect on this vehicle.

Spraying the Final Topcoat CONTINUED

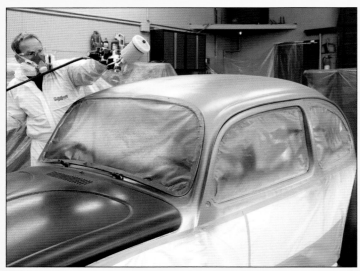

2 Follow your rendering to apply the topcoat color. My spray technique here is not what I typically do on a complete paint job. Just like the red oxide primer, I'm leaving large thin places where I want the underlying layers exposed. Our rendering is a great guide, and by following it, I know I won't need a lot of coverage in the middle or the top of any panel.

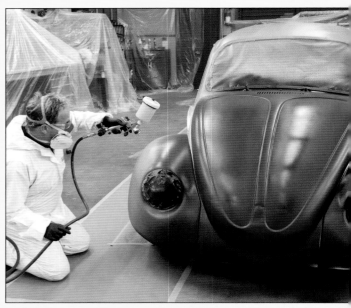

3 Even though my paint strategy is very unconventional here, my paint technique is spot on. Holding the paint gun 6 inches from the panel and moving in a very controlled manner is best. A smooth relaxed pace is essential for controlled paint application.

4 As you spray the last color, visualize where you want worn and faded spots. Remember, the sun fades from the top down.

5 Remember that once the artwork and styling is done, you can spray a flat clearcoat on our paint job to protect it. So, there's no need to excessively layer the color coats.

Unmasking

1 *After another 30 minutes of drying (and another gun cleaning session), you can safely remove the masking paper from the sides and get a closer look of the overall paint scheme.*

2 *When removing masking tape, always pull it against itself to get a clear tape line. Don't risk pulling paint up from the bottom and off of the panel.*

3 *Once the tape is removed, you can see the big picture. For our project, we can see the opacity of the turquoise color on the middle of the hood, under the headlights, and on the roof. Although this looks like a mistake now, it's really an intentional technique that will save us time.*

4 *Remove all of the masking tape and paper to get a better perspective on the next steps. We'll remask later on to clearcoat the entire project for protection.*

Unmasking CONTINUED

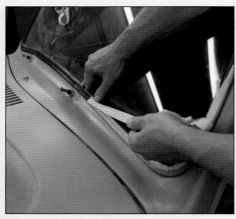

5 If you added a rope under the gaskets, leave it for now in case you want to add detail in these areas.

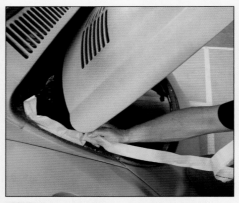

6 If there were an engine here, we'd have spent more time covering up parts and protecting from overspray. This just got the seal covered, since that's all that's really there.

7 Our headlights have plenty of overspray on them from previous paint jobs; nevertheless, we taped ours carefully, so we can control what we do and the outcome of our paint job. Some overspray may look like dirt or age, so we'll leave what's there alone.

8 Even though we're going for an antique look, we still want to be safe and legal. Details, such as the license plate lamp, need to be masked off for safety's sake.

9 We've got a plan for the original (poorly painted) door handles, but the openings in the panels needed to be masked up to protect the interior from overspray. This is still a professional paint job, just an unconventional one.

Aging the Paint

1 To start aging paint and exposing layers, use 400-grit sandpaper and carefully remove the layers f paint according to your taste and strategy.

2 Use a soft sanding block to get an even pattern. Not using some sort of interface pad can cause finger grooves and patterns to emerge in your layers. This process needs to be as even as possible.

3 At this point, you want to stop every few minutes and inspect what you've exposed. It doesn't take uch to go too far and ruin a realistic look. Less is more, nd you can always remove more paint later.

4 For thin vertical surfaces, such as the door post, it is okay to use fingertips to sand, since they're about as wide as the panel is. This is where someone would most likely grab the door to open or close it, so we can sand more and show more wear here.

Aging the Paint CONTINUED

5 Next, sand with a red scuffing pad. This pad gives a subtler pattern and takes off less material. On this panel, we're assuming this car has been sitting with the driver's side against the morning sun for many years. This gives us a backstory for the aging we want to show.

6 Stop and start on several panels, taking many breaks to look at your progress. You want authentic fade, and that takes careful consideration.

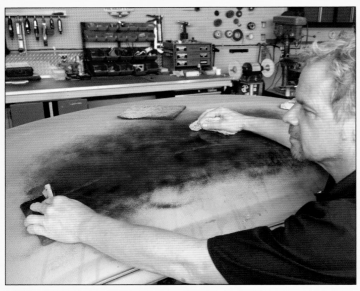

7 Roof panels always have the most sun damage. In our case, we're revealing the red oxide almost out to the edges of the panel. The black ground coat showing signifies that we're almost through to bare metal under the factory sealer in our backstory.

8 We can show sun damage and rust a couple of ways. One way is to use the dual-action sander with the interface pad and 320-grit sandpaper on our rear (fiberglass) fenders, which removes layers nicely and reveals the red oxide quickly.

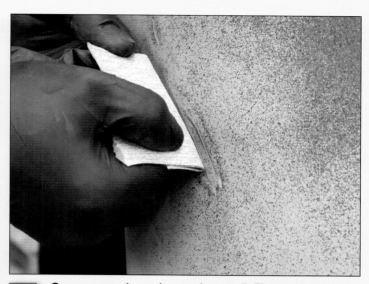

9 Clean the sanding residue with glass cleaner often to check your progress. I've revealed a nice gradual transition from green to red to a little exposed black.

10 Gouges can be enhanced as well. There were some gouges in the fiberglass fender from careless storage of this car. Rather than sand them smooth like we would have when prepping for a conventional paint job, we simply scuffed into the scratches with a red pad and painted over top. Now, the scratches are revealed as the layers are removed. I'll prep inside the scratches with 320-grit sandpaper folded to create a knife's edge.

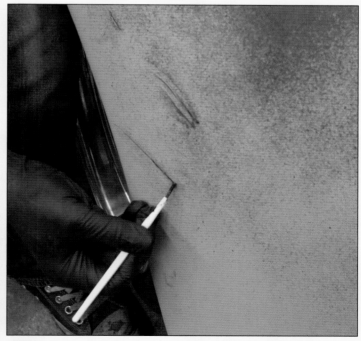

11 To simulate surface rust, use the metal effects iron primer. Dob it on to the exposed ground coat with a modeling brush.

12 Carefully brush the metal primer into the deep gouges, simulating a deep scratch that has gone down to bare metal.

Aging the Paint CONTINUED

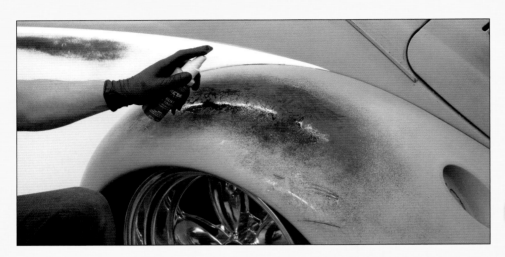

13 Once the rusting primer is applied and allowed to fully dr spray the activator onto the surfaces

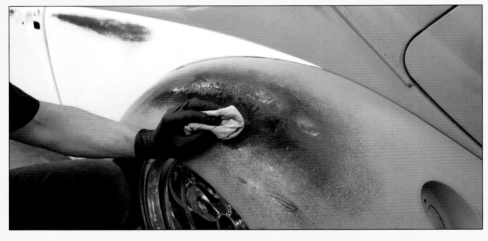

14 Blot the surface to remove the excess activator so that it wor leave streaks in the paint after it drie If it doesn't have iron to oxidize, the activator leaves a crusty white resid after the moisture evaporates.

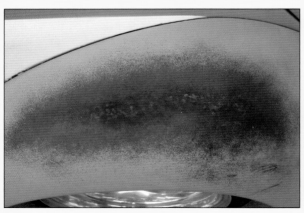

15 After about 15 minutes, the rust starts to show itself. It will continue to get richer in color. Who knew that fiberglass could rust?

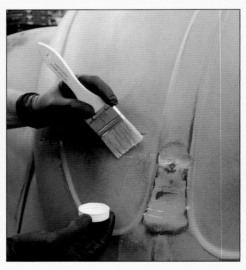

16 If there are dents, add rusting prime to chipped areas to enhance them. There we convenient dents in the front of the hood of our vehicle, so we used a dry brush to add white paint, simulating where the vehicle impacted anothe object and giving anothe layer of realism. I've selectively added rusting primer to chipped areas on the dents as well.

Simulating Bubbling Rust

1 *Many factors determine how panels rust, but I wanted to simulate bubbling rust on the lower edges of several panels, just like in this picture. This is another Volkswagen Beetle from a northern state that has seen some rough winters. Keeping a computer in the shop while styling is a good idea because it often provides inspiration and references for realism.*

2 *To simulate rust that has bubbled up under paint, mix body filler with fiberglass resin. The resin allows the filler to flow and self-level a little. I'm taping off a small crescent area to simulate where the paint has completely delaminated from the metal. Dobbing the runny filler in a pattern around the tape similar to my photo gives me a realistic pattern of rust bubbles. Bridging over the tape edge will give me a peeling-paint edge.*

3 *Let the filler dry for 5 minutes before removing the tape. This will ensure that the filler stays behind. Test with your thumbnail to see when the filler feels rubbery.*

Simulating Bubbling Rust CONTINUED

4 Peel the tape against itself and to the side to remove it from under the overlapped filler, creating a gap.

5 This shows the foundation of my bubbling rust. The rest is simple and depends on your taste and styling.

6 With my bubble strategy locked in, I chose several areas on the vehicle to style. All of the areas are in a similar location to the photo I've been emulating.

7 Use the same process of dobbing filler over tape and paint here. Remember, all of the painted surfaces have been abraded so the filler should have no problem adhering permanently.

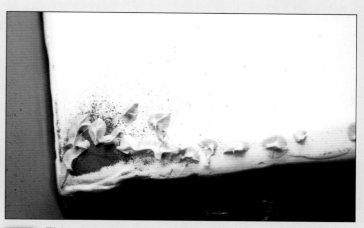

8 *Five minutes later, pull off the tape and create the delaminated paint section. I found that it was best to only do one section at a time so I could pull the tape up at exactly the right time on every area.*

9 *This shows the dried filler without tape. It's not very realistic! Sanding the filler smooth is necessary to round the blobs of filler.*

10 *Using 220-grit sandpaper to smooth and round out the filler blobs so that they become dome-shaped.*

11 *After 220-grit paper, go back over the filler with a red pad to refine the scratches and smooth everything more.*

Simulating Bubbling Rust CONTINUED

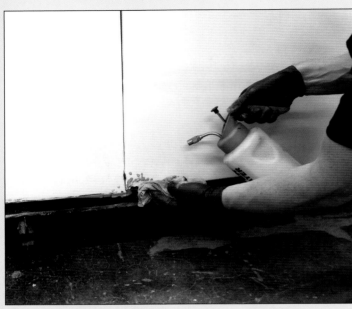

12 *Wipe the sanding dust off with wax and grease remover to prep for paint and primers. Remember that naphtha is a good substitute for body shop grease remover.*

13 *Blot the metal effects primer onto the areas under the filler blobs and wherever you feel like you should see rust forming on the panel.*

14 *Once you are happy with the rust placement, wait for at least 15 minutes for the primer to dry before spritzing on the activator. This is critical to the oxidation process happening properly.*

15 *With some overmix from the full paint job, use a modeling brush to touch up and splotch white paint over the filler blobs and in between rusting primer. This gives a beautiful degraded look.*

16 The air inlet grill on the front is another opportunity to show age and wear. Sand down to the red oxide coating to show actual rust in some places between the grates.

17 This angle shows where to apply the rusting primer: only on the insides of the grates. This is a subtle but realistic touch, based on a real sample I saw in a salvage yard.

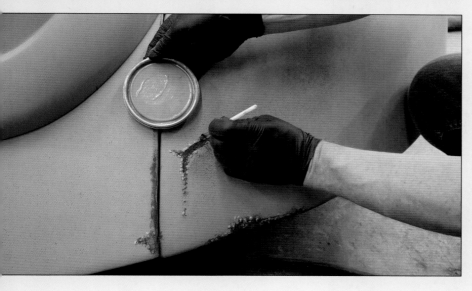

18 Our other opportunity to show how we can simulate rust on fiberglass comes at the expense of some damage to the rear fender from years of abuse. The fiberglass is broken and cracked, but our goal is to make it look dented and rusted through. We used the same filler technique as on the sheet metal, followed by rusting primer, and finally touch-up paint from the green topcoat blotted in with a brush.

Detailing and Aging the Trim

1 We've got a head start with th[e] 1939 Ford-styled taillights, b[u]t the trim is stainless steel in very nice condition. Using red scuffing pads t[o] abrade the surface and remove the gloss on trim.

2 The lenses already show beautiful patina and pitted ru[st] on the chrome ring surrounding the blue dots. We'll just copy this effect[!]

3 With rusting primer loaded into a detail spray gun, remove the air cap off the fluid tip to create a stippling effect.

4 Test your pattern before spraying the project. Our test shows us a nice splatter pattern that will simulated pitted rust.

5 With the gun roughly 6 inches away from the chrome pieces[,] splatter until you have a random pattern of primer splatter. Notice we're also doing the headlight rings and eyebrows, which have also bee[n] scuffed with a red pad to remove the chrome gloss.

6 Leave the primer to dry for 15 to 20 minutes, and then apply the activator. It takes 10 to 15 minutes for the acid to rust the iron in the primer. We installed the parts on to the car to check the effect.

7 The door handles had been sandblasted and painted body color with the last paint job. We used aircraft paint remover and a wire brush to remove the paint and expose the blasted chrome handle, which looked wonderfully aged from that process.

8 The front view of our vehicle is sad, worn out, and shows amazing character! The newly rusted chrome eyelids are period correct for vintage Volkswagens, and our accentuated dents and rust streaks look authentic and realistic.

Detailing and Aging the Trim CONTINUED

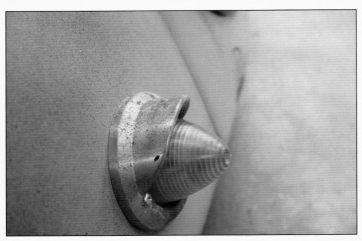

9 The signal lights look particularly great, since they are smaller and easier to scuff to a dull gloss. The lenses were scuffed with a red pad as well, making it difficult to remember that these were brand-new out of the package an hour earlier.

10 The retro-styled taillight bezels take on the appearance of pitted rusty chrome thanks to stippling with the rusting paint and scuffing off the gloss. The blue-dot lenses were a free bonus that show a trend that was huge in the 1950s and 1960s, and they've naturally aged as well.

11 We media-blasted the plastic vents for the quarter panels and blotched rusting primer over the entire vent. Volkswagen people will know that these panels can't ever rust since they're plastic, but in the spirit of fauxtina, we're going to rust them anyway!

12 These vents pop back into the side panels and will continue to rust.

Final Airbrushing

1 You will use the airbrush to add a final layer of styling to the paint job. Rust streaks are easy to create with an airbrush, and the Inspire Base Kit gives us all the colors we need to create our own perfect rust tone, starting with orange.

2 Add black to the orange paint to create a mud brown color. These colors are ready to shoot and only require shaking up.

3 A few drops of red give that oxide tone to our mud brown. Combine that with equal parts of reducer to produce a diluted color that is easy to use and very forgiving.

4 Karajen Corps has a magnetic airport workstation that is perfect for gun and paint storage. You can roll it around the vehicle as you patina all of the panels.

5 Water follows gravity and flows downward. Rust needs water to live! With this in mind, it's easy to find places to style with rust streaks.

Final Airbrushing CONTINUED

6 *A beautiful touch to the fake-rusting plastic vents is a rusty streak coming off the bottom edge.*

7 *The door handles are another opportunity for patina. This effect shows the importance of the practice techniques in chapter 7.*

8 *Fuel makes stains on white paint. Simulate a fuel stain inside the filler door pocket and slightly outside and below.*

9 *Use masking tape to protect the weather seal and create another rust streak and stain under the windshield. This would look awkward and fake if done on the top corner.*

10 *Pull more stains off of dented, rusty rock chips on the hood for a cool and subtle touch.*

11 *The combination of the rust stains overtop of red oxide sanded and exposed layers that give way to the black ground coat that is tinted with actual rust gives sense of realism that is very effective.*

2 *The last thing to do is remove the nylon rope from the window seals. This will let the seals relax against the paint and give the illusion of an original paint job with no overlapping or bridged paint.*

13 *Pull the rope gently and lift it slightly away from the paint so you don't scratch the finish.*

Protecting Patina

If you want to allow nature and time to continue what you started, you may want to just leave your sanded, prepped, and styled paint job in the hands of time and atmosphere. If you want to seal the job and lock it into place, there are a few ways to reach that goal.

There are many ways to protect the art you've created in your patina paint job. Products such as Eastwood's Patina Preserver is one option, although this product works better on smaller projects simply due to the small fluid load in the aerosol can and the large job of coating an entire vehicle. A better option might be to spray a conventional clearcoat over the entire paint job. This would require

remasking the vehicle to protect from overspray on glass, wheels, bumpers, and other items that you want to protect.

Most clearcoats, even matte finish or flat clearcoats, will slightly change the appearance of the color of your project due to the way light reflects off a coating rather than off of the prepped surfaces. In chapter 8, we chose to clearcoat the entire door to protect the sign painting project as well as to cover some sanding scratches below the letters that were caused from a small repair we did with sandpaper. If you plan on driving your vehicle on a regular basis, or simply want the security that your details will not be disturbed or damaged by the elements or wear, then a clear layer of protection is a wise decision.

We've found that a layer of clearcoat over the rusting paint changes the rust from an authentic orange hue to a darker bronze appearance. It also detracts slightly from the realistic look of the uncoated primer. To battle this, you could reapply sections of the primer on top of your clear layer to retain the actual rusted surfaces, but this obviously requires extra steps, time, and materials. For our paint job, we're going to let nature take our fauxtina to the next wonderful stage of degradation by allowing it to naturally oxidize and change over time.

Patina is an ongoing process, and we're curious to see what changes might occur and how our home-crafted version of aging will blend in with exposure to the persistent effects of time.

RECOVERING FROM MISTAKES

In my experience, mistakes are the ultimate teacher. I've always said that the difference between a painter and a paint gun owner is your ability to get yourself out of trouble. Mistakes *always* happen, but there's no such thing as not being able to recover from them, even if that means a respray. A friend told me many years ago, "Kevin, it ain't messed up until you can't fix it no more."

A clear understanding of the paint and the materials that you're working with will help you manage any obstacle that may come up during your paint project. Each paint product comes with a technical data sheet (TDS) that contains information regarding mix ratios, drying times, equipment requirements, and surface compatibility. I have an extensive library of TDS sheets that I refer to with every job, whether it's fauxtina or conventional refinishing.

Have your TDS on hand while you're spraying and follow the rules of the chemistry. Chances are you won't have any issues or problems. The other liberating truth regarding patina is that the mistakes and flaws can and will add to the overall effe of fauxtina, enhancing the appea ance of the project by providin character.

Correcting Masking Errors

Errors can be found after unmas ing layers. Although you can prol ably incorporate these errors in your patina, the goal is to have th illusion of an original-paint patin A blow-through would not have le the factory assembly line, and yo can correct these mistakes.

Correcting Masking Errors

1 *With the final topcoats of paint covering our styling layers, we noticed a couple of things that we didn't plan on after unmasking the panels.*

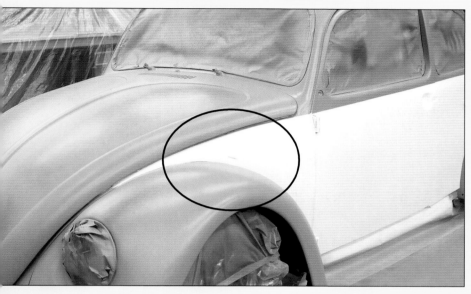

2 If you look closely, you can see where the green topcoat has bled through a gap in the masked off white side panel. This actually happened at the front and rear of the car. Although we could probably incorporate this into our patina, we wanted to have the illusion of an original-paint patina on this car. A blow-through like this would not have left the factory assembly line, so we decided to correct them.

3 This was clearly a mistake in masking. You can tell by the sharp triangle-shaped outline of green on white. There are two coats of color on this, which create a ridge around the outline. There is also as a solid layer of paint to contend with.

4 After letting the paint job sit overnight to thoroughly dry, start by sanding with 600-grit sandpaper that is lubricated with water to keep the paper from clogging.

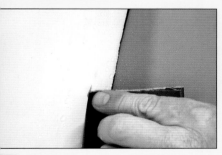

5 Be very careful not to sand outside of the triangle, since ere is a layer of white paint under- eath it that is not very thick. The nger in simply sanding the zone ound the blow-through is that you'll move the white paint around the een overspray and create a notice- le area that is much larger than the iginal anomaly.

6 Once you have sanded off most of the paint, use a gray scuffing pad to gently massage the leftover paint that was in the pores of the coating. Scuffing pads are a wonderful tool that will conform to the inconsistency of the surface. This is an advantage when you want to remove only the very top layer of some paint and don't want to level the surface completely.

7 We've decided to stop at this point, even though there is a slight discoloration at the site of the overspray. This is probably due to sanding through the underlying white coats of paint. Sanding any more will reveal a much darker spot that we didn't consider as our patina plan. The slight discoloration looks more natural and will probably work to our advantage at this point, so we're calling this a success.

Removing Overspray

Overspray happens! If your patina plan allows for a respray or repairs in the backstory, it can actually be a cool effect and detail to leave alone. But overspray on glass is a clear sign that a vehicle has been painted in the aftermarket, since glass is always installed after paint on an automotive assembly line. It takes just a few steps to remove overspray

Removing Overspray

1 *Use a new single-edged razor blade to remove overspray from glass without damaging it. Keep in mind that razor blades dull and nick easily, so using one over and over again can damage glass if the blade itself gets worn out.*

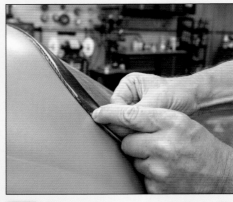

2 *If you use a razor or knife to fix overspray, be very careful not to gouge the fresh paint. Here you can see where our tape job either lifted or didn't cover the rubber seal in the first place. The nylon rope under the seal will keep the glass off the painted body while we repair this flaw easily by simply scraping the paint off the seal with a fingernail.*

3 *A few minutes of focused work is all that is needed to have a perfectly clean rubber seal again.*

4 *We couldn't get our nylon rope underneath the side glass of this car, so we just masked the seals off. There were several places on each side glass where paint bled through the masking job, so there's repair to do here as well. Slip a plastic spreader under the edge of the window seal to protect the body from the blade.*

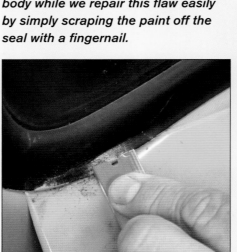

5 *Even when your rubber seals are soft, it takes some time and patience to remove paint without damaging the seal.*

6 *Once all the paint is scraped off the rubber, use a soft towel and acetone to clean the pores of the rubber and restore the look of the seal. Use a lot of care not to let the acetone drip onto the fresh paint! It will reflow the paint layers since they don't have a catalyst!*

Correcting Oversanding

Sanding through the layers of paint into the contrasting colored undercoats is primarily the way to manifest age onto a paint job. It creates the illusion of a weathered paint job that has suffered under UV exposure for decades. One must use care and strategy when sanding to expose layers because you can never sand paint back on that has been removed. To a certain extent, there is no going back.

Remembering the recipe and paint-layer strategy and using your TDS library, you can easily figure out how to spot in a repair, recreating certain layers and sections of your paint job. Part of the appeal of this type of paint job is that if the color match is off a little, it adds character. If it looks like it has been patched over with paint at some point in its life, it adds history and a backstory that might be interesting.

Repairing Oversanding

1 While I was sanding through the layers on the top of the Volkswagen, I sanded more of the green topcoat off than I intended. I wanted a green halo of paint around the perimeter of the roof and sun-faded layers of the red oxide and black ground coat. I simply sanded too much turquoise off for the look I was after.

4 You may need to blend in the new color more. The new layer looked very bright compared to everything around it. After 15 minutes of drying time, I was able to run a red scuffing pad over the repair area, which muted the color and brought out more of the green tone that the surrounding area has.

2 To spot in, load a detail spray gun with a couple of ounces of paint for the repair. Set the fluid control knob so there is a small amount of paint coming out as you pull the trigger.

3 Make as many passes as you need to add color. I made a total of four passes over the sanded transition of color, taking my time not to spray any farther into the panel and to stay on the edge.

Repairing Oversanding CONTINUED

5 *Use a glass cleaner and a clean towel to wipe all the sanding residue from the scuffing pad off the panel and check the blend.*

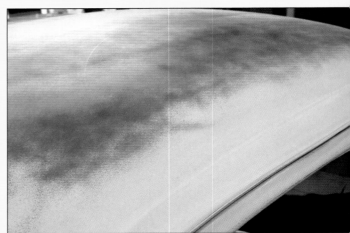

6 *The blend is successful. I've restored the look of an even fade rather than a totally degraded panel, which follows my patina plan.*

Letter Correction

1 *One of the stencils on our sign painting project lifted as we were spraying the letter color. This may have been due to the rough surface we had to work on or simply not pressing the stencil down around the letter edge. Regardless, there's blow-through at the bottom of the letter. We're emulating the look of hand-lettered, brush-painted letters on this door, so overspray would diminish our realistic effect.*

2 *Since we coated the door of the truck with two coats of a flat clearcoat before starting the lettering project, we know there was a barrier to work against without digging into the original patina of the vintage paint. Carefully sanding around the letter solved our problem, and since we sanded the letters and the pin-striped drop shadows later as well, the overall look is that of a degraded old sign-painting job that has a realistic and period-correct look. However, there are still visible sanding scratches in the undercoat of clear beneath the letters.*

Correcting Runs

Runs in paint happen when a layer is overcoated, typically due to bad technique, improper gun settings, or improperly blended paint chemistry. Surfacing down runs to flatten them out is a very simple concept, and repairing a run in the paint is a simple procedure, providing there is enough material to do the repair.

The liberating part of fauxtina is that a run in the paint is actually a character sign and can be a benefit of the paint job, not a problem to fix. Realism is the goal, and mistakes happen in real life. Every flaw has a story behind it, and it's your job creating the patina to expose the story, or at least open the mind of some-

body looking at the car to invent their own backstory.

Coverups

When a tattoo artist is asked to cover up another artist's work, it's referred to as a cover-up tattoo. The artist needs to use colors and line detail to develop a new perception of the art, and one that removes any hint of the underlying artwork. Correcting patina can be exactly the same.

Understanding the recipe of layers that you've laid down will give you a great way to correct the fauxtina finish at any or every stage. If you've sanded too far and exposed too much of an underlying layer, you can reapply the different colors in the correct

order and simply start again! Mistakes give character, but they're also easy to repair. As you go through some of the exercise, you'll find that you can easily correct mistakes, and that in doing just that there may be more opportunities to create your version of patina.

So if mistakes are the ultimate teacher, and this style of painting actually embraces mistakes in all of their flawed beauty, the reality is there is no such thing as a mistake. Knowing that should feel great! Being able to correct and refine your patina plan is quite simple, and if you arm yourself with basic skills, a plan of action, and an open mind that will see opportunity instead of a misstep, you'll be able to turn around any deviation in your plan, and turn it into a success.

3 *Spraying another coat of clear over all of our artwork filled in the sanding scratches around the letters, making them completely disappear. That is also the beauty and strategy of planning a final coat of clear on the entire patina job if there are details like this that you want to correct.*

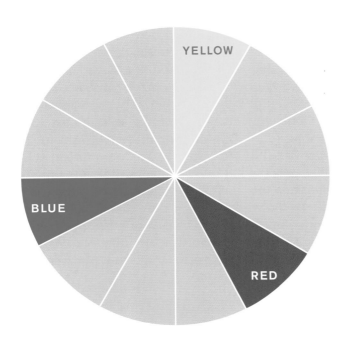

PRIMARY COLORS

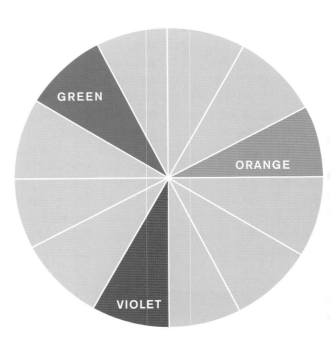

SECONDARY COLORS

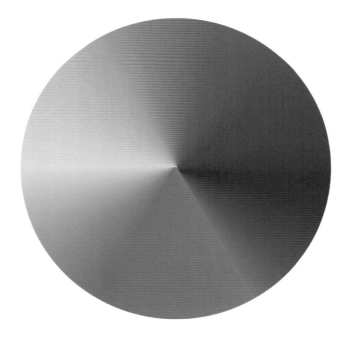

COLOR WHEEL

eneral Supplies Needed for Patina
gallon plastic buckets
-hp pump, a 60-gallon air storage
 tank
erosol primers
ellophane
leaning supplies
isposable paint brushes called chip
 brushes
rop cloths
loves
ravity-fed airbrush and a high-
volume, low-pressure (HVLP) gun
terface pad
acquer thinner
asking paper
asking tape
atte clearcoat
on-catalyzed paints
paint roller designed for latex paint
astic cups
neumatic spray equipment
rotective clothing
espiratory equipment
afety glasses
andpaper or scuffing pads
cale
ngle-edge razor blades
ponges
ainless cups
ir sticks
rainers
c rag

notographs
SLR camera or cellphone camera
kjet printer

Iding Rust
stilled vinegar
ravity-fed airbrush

Scuffing pads
Touch-up brushes

To Age Paint
Base coat
Finish coat
Primer
Sandpaper or scuffing pad (400 and
 600 grit)
Solvent-based cleaner

Accelerated Rusting
Ammonia
Chip brush
Distilled vinegar
Iodized table salt
Plastic mixing pails
A plastic spoon
Patina preserver spray

Faster Accelerated Rusting
180-grit sandpaper
Chip brush
Oxidizing iron primer
Rust activating spray
Catalyzed paint

Aging Plastic
220-grit sandpaper
Black craft paint
Elmer's wood glue
Model builders' glue
Red, grey, and white scuffing pads

Aging Glass
600-grit sandpaper
1500-grit sandpaper
Airbrush compressor
Detail-etching airbrush
Dual-action sander
Highlighter pen

Model builders' glue
Soft interface pad

Aging Chrome
Gravity-fed airbrush
Rusting metallic primer
Sandblast cabinet or gun
Scuffing pads

Tools for Airbrushing
Airbrush workstation
Compressed air source
Dropper
Gravity-fed brush with a removable
 top
Inline moisture filter
Paint cup and cap
Protective cover for the brush air cap
Push-style air fitting
Regulator
Standard airbrush air hose
Wrench for disassembly and assembly

Creating Vintage Signage
400-grit sandpaper
1000-grit sandpaper
1-Shot enamel
1-Shot striping paint
Aerosol spray paint
Air compressor
Automotive masking paper
Camel hair striping brushes
China marker
Drop cloths
Grey scuffing pad
Ground coat of matte clear
High-volume, low-pressure (HVLP) gun
Reducer
Ruler
Mineral spirits
Self-adhesive stencils

Auto Body Toolmart
2545 Millennium Drive
Elgin IL, 60124
800-382-1200
autobodytoolmart.com

Campbell Hausfeld Tools
100 Production Drive
Harrison, OH 45030
800-543-6400
campbellhausfeld.com

Custom Paints
13140 Spring Hill Drive
Spring Hill, FL 34609
727-857-7885
custompaints.com

Dupli-Color
800-247-3270
duplicolor.com

Eastwood Company
263 Shoemaker Road
Pottstown, PA 19464
800-343-9353
eastwood.com

Mack Striping Brushes
216 East Chicago Street
Jonesville, MI 49250
517-849-9272
mackbrush.com

Norton Abrasives
One New Bond Street
Worcester, MA 01606
254-918-2313
nortonabrasives.com

1-Shot Paints
760 Pittsburgh Drive
Delaware, OH 43015
800-323-6593
1shot.com

Paintucation Instructional Videos
1203 Bear Creek Pike
Columbia, TN 38401
931-388-3531
info@paintucation.com
paintucation.com

3M Corporate Headquarters
3M Center
St. Paul, MN 55144-1000
888-364-3577
3M.com

U-POL Automotive Supplies
108 Commerce Way
Easton, PA 18040
610-746-7081
u-pol.com